Starting Out With

NATIVES

Starting Out With

NATIVES

EASY-TO-GROW PLANTS

FOR YOUR AREA

JOHN WRIGLEY
MURRAY FAGG

First published in Australia in 2002 by Reed New Holland
an imprint of New Holland Publishers (Australia) Pty Ltd
Sydney • Auckland • London • Cape Town

1/66 Gibbes Street Chatswood NSW 2067 Australia
218 Lake Road Northcote Auckland 0627 New Zealand
Garfield House 86–88 Edgware Road London W22EA United Kingdom
Wembley Square First Floor Solan Road Gardens Cape Town 8001 South Africa

Reprinted in 2002, 2003 (twice), 2004, 2005, 2006, 2007, 2012

National Library of Australia Cataloguing-in-Publication Data:

Wrigley, John W. (John Walter).
Starting out with natives : easy-to-grow plants for your area.

Includes index.
ISBN 9781876334666 (pbk.).

1. Native plant gardening - Australia. 2. Wild flower
gardening - Australia. I. Fagg, Murray. II. Title.

635.95194

Publisher: Louise Egerton
Project Editor: Yani Silvana
Editor: Anne Savage
Designer: Alix Korte
Cover Design: Alix Korte
Cartographer: Ian Faulkner
Production Controller: Wendy Hunt
Reproduction: Sang Choy International, Singapore
Printer: Craft Print International Ltd, Singapore

Contents

Introduction

Growing native plants is easy. If you select the right species for your area and follow a few simple rules, you should have no problems. This book has been written to set you on the right track. As native plants in general prefer well-drained soil, it is also recommended that if your garden soil is heavy loam or clay, you should improve the drainage by building up the garden beds to about 30 cm high with a mixture of sandy soil and compost or leaf litter.

• Cheer up a permanently damp area with the sunny flowers of the Common Buttercup.

• Some boronias are reputedly difficult to grow, but Keys' Boronia is fairly hardy.

· Choosing a Plant

Many of the plants mentioned in this book are available from general nurseries. For some, however, you may have to visit a specialist native plant nursery. These are located in most major centres but if you have difficulty in finding one, contact your local Australian Plants Society. Contact addresses are given on page 11. Always ensure that the plant you choose is healthy and growing vigorously. Its roots should not be protruding from the holes in the base of the pot.

◄ The Tasman Flax Lily is a hardy and adaptable plant for almost any type of soil.

· Planting

Note whether your plant requires full sun or some shade and choose its position carefully. If the soil has not been used for some time, it will be hard, so dig the ground for about 30 cm around the planting position to allow the roots to penetrate the soil easily. Prepare a hole a little larger than the pot size and carefully up-end the plant and remove the container. Place the plant in the hole and fill in around it with the loose soil. The soil level around the plant should be the same as when it was in the pot. Firm the soil around the plant with your hands and water well.

• Climatic Zones

Below is a map of Australia showing the various climatic zones of the country. It is important that you note the zone in which you live and select species marked as suitable for that region.

• Maintenance

For the first few weeks, make sure the plant does not dry out. After that, water should only be required in really dry or hot weather. If

• Straw Flowers, or Everlasting Daisies, provide a beautiful rockery display in spring.

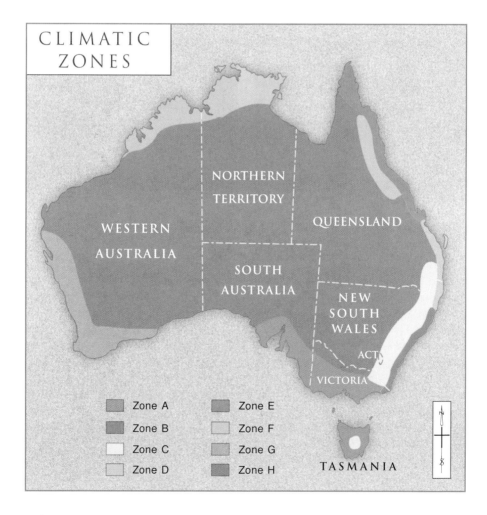

CLIMATIC
ZONES

NORTHERN
TERRITORY

QUEENSLAND

WESTERN
AUSTRALIA

SOUTH
AUSTRALIA

NEW
SOUTH
WALES

ACT

VICTORIA

Zone A   Zone E

Zone B   Zone F

Zone C   Zone G

Zone D   Zone H

TASMANIA

watering is necessary, leave the hose in position long enough to ensure that the water penetrates deeply into the soil. Light watering by hand only encourages surface roots to develop and these will quickly dry out.

Mulching is important to conserve moisture. Mulch may be made of leaf litter, compost, wood chips or tea tree — all are suitable. As well as conserving moisture, a mulch inhibits weed growth and tends to maintain an even temperature in the topsoil.

• Water Gums are useful for damp spots and are good shade trees for small gardens. Their yellow flowers attract insects.

Native plants do appreciate fertiliser, despite the many stories that say they do not need it. This belief arose because many of our most beautiful native plants grow on soils that are low in phosphorus, and have developed a root system that allows them to use the small quantities available to the maximum. Consequently, when high phosphorus fertilisers are used on them, they are unable to cope with the amount of phosphorus and they die. Use only fertilisers that are formulated specifically for natives or look for fertilisers that have a nitrogen (N),

phosphorus (P), potassium (K) ratio of about 10:3:6. Multigro® is one such product.

Native plants will also accept pruning. This is best done after flowering and when the plant is about to start growing new shoots. This may be in late spring for mild or warm coastal areas or early summer for colder regions. There can be several reasons for pruning. Perhaps your plant has become too large for the position it is in, or straying branches have caused it to develop an ungainly shape. Long branches may be removed by carefully cutting just above a leaf node. Tip prune by removing just a few centimetres from most of the branches to encourage further branching and the development of a rounded shape. This method usually improves flower production for the following year.

Most native plants do not take kindly to being moved, however. Should it be necessary to transplant a mature shrub, prune the plant heavily by taking off at least two-thirds of the branches. Using a sharp spade, cut around the plant to a depth of about 30 cm, making a circle of at least 50 cm diameter. Have the new hole ready to receive your plant, ensuring that the soil is moist. Carefully remove the pruned plant, keeping as much soil around the roots as possible. If it is to be moved any distance, it is advisable to wrap the root ball tightly in hessian. Carefully place the plant in the new hole after removing the hessian. Fill in the soil firmly around it and water well. Don't allow the plant to dry out over the next few weeks.

• Cultivars

'Cultivar' is a shorthand term for 'cultivated variety'. It may be a specially selected form of a natural species or it may be the result of intentional hybridisation (or crossing) between two species that has produced a plant with some characteristics of both its parents. Hybridisation of exotic species, such as roses, has been in progress for hundreds of years, giving us the wonderful blooms with which we are familiar. Breeding of native cultivars has become popular in recent years and has resulted in some very fine plants. When you go to a nursery today, you will find many native plants with fancy names like 'Honey Gem', 'Golden Yu-lo', 'Pink Cascade', 'White Lace', 'Regal Claw'. These are cultivars that have been bred or specially selected for superior horticultural characteristics. *Grevillea* 'Honey Gem' is a hybrid between *Grevillea pteridifolia* and *G. banksii*, resulting in a plant that flowers for most of the year with wonderful orange flowers that attract nectar-seeking birds; *Melaleuca* 'White Lace' is a specially selected white-flowering form of *M. thymifolia*. Such plants are often very hardy and usually make excellent garden subjects.

· Plant Names

If you are beginning to grow native plants you may be a little wary of the long Latin names on plant labels. These are used by botanists to distinguish one species from another. The first name is the genus name and the second is the species name. For instance, if we take *Grevillea robusta*, the Silky Oak, *Grevillea* is the name of the genus, which includes more than 300 species, and *robusta* is just one species of this large genus. You could liken this to your own name, where your family name is the genus and your first name is the species name. Botanic names give some stability to the naming of plants; once a plant has been described (named) by a botanist in a scien-

• Lilly Pilly, an easy-to-grow rainforest plant, grows well near the sea. It has glossy leaves and produces attractive, edible fruits.

tific journal, this name is accepted throughout the world. However, sometimes further botanic research produces evidence that necessitates a change of name and the original name becomes a synonym.

Most familiar exotic garden plants have been in cultivation for many years and have generally accepted common names — for instance, we know *Antirrhinum* as a snapdragon. Australian native plants, on the other hand, have a relatively recent history of cultivation and in many cases common names have not become well established. This has resulted in different common names being used in different areas for the same species and, in some cases, the same common name being used for several different plants. In this book we have attempted to use the common name wherever possible, but have always associated it with the plant's botanic name to avoid confusion.

The plants have been grouped under general headings such as Annuals, Bottlebrushes, Feather Flowers or Kangaroo Paws and Their Relatives. You can search for a particular plant either on the Contents page or in the Index.

Australian Plants Society

The Australian Plants Society is an organisation with State societies loosely linked by a national body known as The Association of Australian Plants Societies. If you are having trouble locating plants mentioned in this book, contact your State group for further information. They will have details of specialist native plant nurseries your area. Contact addresses are given below, along with their web sites.

National web site: http://farrer.riv.csu.edu.au/ASGAP/

Australian Plants Online (quarterly online magazine)
http://farrer.riv. csu.edu.au/ASGAP/apoline.html

Australian Plants Society (NSW)
Secretary: Joanne Caldwell, 33 Wymah Crescent
    Berowra Heights NSW 2082
http://www.austplants-nsw.org.au/

The Society for Growing Australian Plants, Canberra Region Inc.
Secretary: Morris Duggan, PO Box 217
    Civic Square ACT 2608
http://www.anbg.gov.au/sgap/

Australian Plants Society (SGAP Victoria) Inc.
Secretary: PO Box 357 Hawthorn Vic 3122
http://home.vicnet.net.au/~sgapvic/

Australian Plants Society, SA Region Inc.
Secretary: Michael Freeborn, PO Box 304
    Unley SA 5076
http://members.iweb.net.au/~sgap/

Wildflower Society of Western Australia, Inc.
Secretary: Barbara Dewar, PO Box 64
    Nedlands WA 6009
http://www.ozemail.com.au/~wildflowers/

The Society for Growing Australian Plants (Queensland) Inc.
Secretary: Ian Waldron, PO Box 586
    Fortitude Valley Qld 4006
http://www.sgapqld.org.au

Australian Plants Society Tasmania Inc.
Secretary: PO Box 75 Exeter Tas 7275
http://www.trump.net.au/~joroco/sgaptas-index.htm

The Australian Carnivorous Plant Society, Inc.
Also sells seeds of native carnivorous plants to members: PO Box 391 St Agnes SA 5097
http://www.acps.org.au

ADDITIONAL USEFUL WEB SITES

Australian National Botanic Gardens
http://www.anbg.gov.au/anbg/

Australian Native Plant Nurseries
http://farrer.csu.edu/ASGAP/nursery.html

Sydney Wildflower Nursery West
http://www.nativenursery.com.au/SWNWest

Zanthorrea Nursery, Perth
http://tnet.com.au/~zan/

Fairhill Nursery, Queensland
http://fairhillnursery.com/index.html

Kuranga Nursery, Melbourne
http://www.kuranga.com.au

Plants of Sydney
http://users.bigpond.net.au/filejest/index.html

Oz Natives
http://www.growinglifestyle.com/hand46/garden/native/

Annuals

 An annual completes its life cycle in one year. Spring- and summer-flowering annuals are usually planted in late winter in warm coastal climates or in early spring, after the threat of frosts is over, in cooler areas. By late spring to early summer flowering is at its peak, and by mid- to late summer the plants are setting seed. Most annuals prefer a sunny location. Lots of well-rotted compost or old animal or fowl manure, or a feed of Dynamic Lifter®, will give the plants a good start. There are a number of native annuals available as seeds from commercial seed suppliers and sold by chain store gardening departments or nurseries. They are occasionally available in punnets of seedlings. Direct sow seeds into well-prepared soil and cover with fine sandy soil, or sow into punnets where they are easier to look after. Plant out seedlings when they are 10–15 cm high. You can mass-plant, create borders or dot around other plants in a rockery to provide spots of colour through spring and summer. Water well.

Rock Isotome • *Isotoma axillaris*   *All Zones*

This frost-hardy plant, 30 cm high, produces masses of light blue five-petalled flowers in late spring and summer. The dainty foliage is much divided. It often drops seed which germinates the following season, making it useful for rockeries. Watch out for the sap, which may irritate your eyes if you rub them with your finger. Collect seed towards the end of the flowering period. Small, green, almost shapeless grubs sometimes cause defoliation. Control with any caterpillar pesticide.

Rottnest Island Daisy • *Trachymene caerulea*   *All Zones*

This taller summer-flowering annual gives a wonderful display. The blooms make fine cut flowers. Well-grown plants reach 80 cm high. Pinch out the growing tips of young plants to encourage branching. Each flowerhead, about 5 cm in diameter, is composed of many tiny light blue flowers, rather like a pincushion. (Despite its common name, this plant is more closely related to carrots than to true daisies.)

Straw Flower
or Everlasting Daisy • *Bracteantha bracteata*   *All Zones*

Most of Australia's native annuals are true daisies and this, the best known, is sure to give you a fine display in spring and summer. It is frost hardy and comes in several colours, from yellow to white and shades of red and brown. Plants reach about 40 cm in height. The papery flowers are used fresh or dried.

• Rock Isotome *Isotoma axillaris*

• Rottnest Island Daisy *Trachymene caerulea*

• Straw Flower or Everlasting Daisy *Bracteantha bracteata*

Pink Everlasting · *Rhodanthe manglesii* *All Zones*

This is another paper daisy, like the Straw Flower, worth growing. It requires protection from late frosts. It forms a small bushy plant only about 30 cm high and produces slightly drooping pink flowerheads about 2.5 cm in diameter in spring.

Pink Sunray · *Rhodanthe chlorocephala* ssp. *rosea* *All Zones*

More upright than the Pink Everlasting, and with larger flowers, this paper daisy varies in colour from almost white to deep pink. Grows to 40 cm high. For excellent dried flowers, hang the spring blooms upside down in a dry breezy situation for a few weeks.

Poached Egg Daisy · *Polycalymma stuartii* *All Zones*

Well named for its yellow centre and white papery bracts, this species reaches about 40 cm in height. The leaves are grey-green and often hairy. Full sun is essential for good spring flowering. It is a good bedding plant.

Swan River Daisy · *Brachyscome iberidifolia* *All Zones*

Growing only to about 25 cm high, this daisy produces masses of 2 cm diameter flowers in spring. Flower colours vary from white to blue, mauve and even purple, with yellow or sometimes dark centres. Seeds are often available from supermarkets.

Banksias

While these well-known plants from both sides of the continent make excellent garden specimens, take care to choose the right species for your area. Those from Western Australia are very difficult to grow on the humid east coast and in the tropics. In nature these species experience wet winters and dry summers, and high summer humidity makes them susceptible to fungal diseases. Banksias require well-drained soil and full or near to full sun. Nectar-seeking birds are attracted to the flowers, and most make good cut flowers. Plants are readily available from nurseries. Banksias can also be easily grown from the seeds embedded in the large woody cones that form after flowering. To simulate the effect of bushfire, which releases the seeds in most species, place the cones in the oven at about 120 °C for one hour and the seed follicles will open. Knock out the seeds and sow in pots or punnets. Germination takes four or five weeks.

Heath Banksia · *Banksia ericifolia* Zones: A B C D G

If you need a dense screening plant, Heath Banksia is an ideal choice. A large bushy shrub from the east coast, it grows 3–4 m high and about 4 m across. The large orange flower spikes, up to 25 cm long, are produced in autumn and contrast well against the neat dark green foliage. The hybrid 'Giant Candles' has even larger flower spikes.

• Pink Everlasting *Rhodanthe manglesii*

• Pink Sunray *Rhodanthe chlorocephala* ssp. *rosea*

• Poached Egg Daisy *Polycalymma stuartii*

• Swan River Daisy *Brachyscome iberidifolia*

• Heath Banksia *Banksia ericifolia*

Bull Banksia · *Banksia grandis*   *Zones:* A G H

This western species forms a tree to 10 m, although in exposed coastal areas it becomes more shrub-like. You may have seen its enormous fruiting cones used to make candlesticks or lamp bases. The yellow flower spikes, up to 30 cm long, appear in spring. The large toothed leaves can be used to dramatic effect in floral arrangements.

Firewood Banksia · *Banksia menziesii*   *Zones:* A G H

Common around Perth, where it makes an open, often twisted tree to 6 m. Its beautiful 15 cm flower spikes make up for any lack of shapeliness in the tree. The autumn flowers are pink in bud and open to yellow. This contrast makes the half-opened flowers particularly attractive.

Swamp Banksia · *Banksia robur*   *Zones:* A B C D E G

One of the few banksias that you can position in a damp spot, the Swamp Banksia has large leathery leaves up to 30 cm long and large 17 cm cylindrical flower spikes produced from late summer to winter. These are an unusual green in bud and open to yellow. This is an upright shrub to 2 m that occasionally produces flowers near the base of its stems.

Hairpin Banksia · *Banksia spinulosa*   *Zones:* A B C D E G

This small to medium-sized shrub, which flowers in autumn and winter, is very useful in the garden. Several forms are available, so examine the label when purchasing a specimen to ascertain its ultimate height. A dwarf form named 'Birthday Candles' grows only about 50 cm high by 1 m wide. Others are shrubs up to 1.5 m by 2 m. Flower spikes vary in colour from yellow to deep orange. The flower styles that give the species its common name are sometimes deep red.

Boab Tree

 The sole Australian member of this vigorous genus is a fine specimen tree for large gardens in tropical and warmer subtropical areas. Other species, all with the same swollen trunks, occur in Africa, Madagascar and India.

Boab Tree · *Adansonia gregorii*   *Zones:* F H

This unique deciduous tree from the Kimberley region of Western Australia has an enormous, swollen, bottle-like trunk and will reach 14 m in height. The leaves have seven leaflets and the large white fluffy flowers, about 10 cm in diameter, appear at the start of the wet season as it comes into leaf. Propagate from fresh seed or cut a healthy branch or even a main trunk and place it in the ground. If kept reasonably moist, the cutting will form roots in a few weeks. Frost tender.

• **Bull Banksia** *Banksia grandis*

• **Firewood Banksia** *Banksia menziesii*

• **Swamp Banksia** *Banksia robur*

• **Hairpin Banksia** *Banksia spinulosa*

• **Boab Tree** *Adansonia gregorii*

Boobiallas

Several species of the genus Myoporum *are commonly known as boob-ialla, from the Aboriginal name for one species. The fruits are edible but they are an acquired taste and are probably best left to attract birds. These hardy plants prefer full sun and accept all but wet soils*

Creeping Boobialla · *Myoporum parvifolium*   *Zones:* A B C D H

This is a prostrate plant spreading to 1 m across, which makes an excellent ground cover or rockery plant. It produces clusters of small white five-petalled flowers in spring and summer. It is generally easy to grow, although it is occasionally attacked by scale, which can be controlled with white oil. Moderately frost hardy. Propagate from cuttings.

Weeping Boobialla · *Myoporum floribundum*   *Zones:* A B C G H

This is an open shrub to 3 m high by 3 m across with fine 9 cm leaves drooping from the horizontal stems. Tiny white star-shaped flowers are borne on the upper surface of the branches in spring. Frost hardy. Propagate from cuttings.

Boronias and Their Relatives

Many species of boronia have the reputation of being difficult to cultivate. The species listed here have proved reasonably hardy, provided you give them very good drainage and a thick mulch of leaf litter, and are well worth trying. Prune lightly after flowering. Propagate from cuttings.

Toothed Boronia · *Boronia denticulata*   *Zones:* A B C G

A rounded shrub to about 1 m high by 60 cm across, this Western Australian species has light green toothed leaves and masses of pink star-shaped flowers in spring. Frost hardy.

Keys' Boronia · *Boronia keysii*   *Zones:* A B C D G

Although very rare in nature, this southern Queensland species has proved hardy in cultivation. An open rounded shrub to 1.5 m high, its pink star-shaped flowers appear from early spring to early summer. Prefers a little shade and may not tolerate heavy frosts.

Kalgan · *Boronia heterophylla*   *Zones:* A C G

This Western Australian species is probably the best-known boronia in cultivation. Forming a compact shrub 1.5 m high by 1 m across, its deep pink spring flowers are cup-shaped and wonderfully perfumed. Prefers some shade. Frost hardy.

• Weeping Boobialla *Myoporum floribundum*

• Creeping Boobialla *Myoporum parvifolium*

• Toothed Boronia *Boronia denticulata*

• Keys' Boronia *Boronia keysii*

• Kalgan *Boronia heterophylla*

Pink Star · *Zieria prostrata*   *Zones:* A B C D G

This rare but hardy ground cover, found in the wild only on several northern New South Wales headlands, spreads to 50 cm and has shiny dark green leaves. The small star-shaped pink flowers appear in spring. It enjoys full sun and withstands salt spray.

Bottlebrushes

 Bottlebrushes, members of the genus Callistemon, *are amongst the hardiest of native plants. There are 38 species and many cultivars. You can grow them in almost any soil condition in full sun, and they will reward you with flowers. Birds are attracted to the blossoms, which may be red, cream, white, pink or mauve. They will accept hard pruning, which is best done after their spring flowering period. As most plants purchased from nurseries are cultivars, they will not necessarily come true from seed, so if you want to propagate them, take cuttings in February. Some plants may be attacked by scale or pimple psyllids, which cause lumps to appear on the leaves. Spray with white oil to control them. Sawfly larvae (appearing as a mass of caterpillars) may cause some defoliation. These pests are best knocked to the ground and squashed. The selection of species described below gives the gardener a choice of various colours and forms to create interest in the garden design.*

Endeavour · *Callistemon* 'Endeavour'   *All Zones*

This cultivar forms a dense shrub to 2.5 m high by 2.5 m across with foliage to the ground. Its brilliant red flowers appear at least twice each year, in spring and summer. It makes an attractive screen or hedge. This is one of the most reliable bottebrushes. Frost hardy.

Dawson River Weeper ·
Callistemon 'Dawson River Weeper'   *Zones:* A B D E F G

This very popular large shrub reaches 5 m high by 5 m across, with pendulous branches. The bright red flowers appear in spring and summer flushes and occasionally at other times. It is a little frost tender. Ample watering in dry periods will ensure good flowering and strong growth. It is a favourite plant of lorikeets and the Scarlet Honeyeater.

Pink Champagne · *Callistemon* 'Pink Champagne'   *Zones:* A B D E F G

Forming a tall, slightly open shrub to 3 m high by 2 m across, this cultivar produces delicate pink flowers in spring and summer. Although not as prolific in its flowering as other cultivars, it is well worth growing for its flower colour. It may be affected by heavy frosts.

• Pink Star *Zieria prostrata*

• Endeavour *Callistemon* 'Endeavour'

• Dawson River Weeper *Callistemon* 'Dawson River Weeper'

• Pink Champagne *Callistemon* 'Pink Champagne'

Mauve Mist · *Callistemon* 'Mauve Mist' *All Zones*

Probably the best of the mauve-flowered bottlebrushes, this cultivar forms a dense rounded shrub to 3 m high by 3 m across. Its peak flowering period is summer. It makes an excellent screen plant. Frost hardy.

Pink Tips · *Callistemon salignus* *Zones:* A B D E F G

More a tree than a shrub, this species will reach 12 m in height. It has papery bark and the young growth is pink, hence the common name. The flowers are cream and displayed in spring. Prefers a moist position for best growth but it tolerates drier conditions. It is slightly frost tender.

White Anzac · *Callistemon* 'White Anzac' *All Zones*

This dwarf cultivar forms a spreading shrub 1 m high by 3 m across. It is extremely hardy. The flowers are white and appear in late spring and early summer. This variety is resistant to salt spray so it is ideal for coastal gardens. Frost hardy.

Buttercups

Buttercups belong to the genus Ranunculus, *which includes more than 400 species worldwide, over 40 of them native to Australia. Most have bright yellow open or cup-shaped flowers, but several from alpine areas are white. The leaves are mostly much divided and bright green, contrasting well with the flowers. Most buttercups occur naturally in damp areas and because of this are ideal for growing near water features or in constantly wet soil. You can propagate them by division or from seed.*

Common Buttercup · *Ranunculus lappaceus* *Zones:* A B C D G

This vigorous perennial grows to 40 cm high with branched flowering stems bearing golden yellow, five-petalled, cup-shaped flowers in spring and summer. It is extremely hardy if given a sunny position and ample water. Frost hardy.

Water Buttercup · *Ranunculus inundatus* *Zones:* A B C D G

This little plant is almost prostrate and will grow in water to 15 cm deep or in very wet soil. Its leaves are divided into many very narrow segments and the golden yellow, open flowers with five to nine petals appear in spring and summer. It is also frost hardy. It will grow in full sun or a little shade.

• **Mauve Mist** *Callistemon* 'Mauve Mist'

• **Pink Tips** *Callistemon salignus*

• **Common Buttercup** *Ranunculus lappaceus*

• **White Anzac** *Callistemon* 'White Anzac'

• **Water Buttercup** *Ranunculus inundatus*

Cassias

Cassias mostly occur in the drier parts of Australia although several of the taller species are found in rainforest. Botanists have transferred most of the shrubby species to the genus Senna, but the common name cassia is still generally maintained. The foliage of most species is a feature, with many of the shrubby species having silvery grey leaves that provide an excellent contrast in the garden. Grow in full sun and propagate from seed which has been soaked in boiling water overnight.

Brewster's Cassia · *Cassia brewsteri* var. *brewsteri*   *Zones:* B D E F H
This small bushy tree grows to about 7 m high and may lose its leaves in dry conditions. The orange-yellow to red flowers are borne on pendulous sprays, which may be up to 20 cm long, in spring and early summer. Good drainage is needed and it is frost tender.

Spreading Cassia · *Senna aciphylla*   *Zones:* A B C G
This almost prostrate plant, spreading to 1.5 m, may be used as a ground cover. It has dark green divided foliage and produces bright yellow flowers in spring. It is very frost hardy.

Silver Cassia · *Senna artemisioides*   *Zones:* B F H
Forming a rounded shrub to 2 m, this species has outstanding silver-grey feathery leaves and produces bright yellow flowers in spring. It must have a sunny well-drained position. It is slightly frost tender.

Christmas Bells

There are four species of Christmas bells in Australia, three occurring in New South Wales and one in Tasmania. The best-known species, and the one that is usually grown, occurs in low wet heath on the central and mid-north coast of New South Wales, where the water table is fairly near the surface. Propagation is from seed and plants are often available commercially.

Large-flowered Christmas Bell · *Blandfordia grandiflora*   *Zones:* A B C D
Flowering from early December and often extending to March, this beautiful species varies in flower colour, from red bells with yellow tips, to bells which are all yellow. The bells are up to 6 cm long and are borne in heads of up to 8 or 9 flowers. Seedlings usually flower in the third year if given ample water and planted in sandy soil with reasonable drainage. Full or part sun is best. It makes an excellent cut flower.

• Brewster's Cassia *Cassia brewsteri* var. *brewsteri*

• Spreading Cassia *Senna aciphylla*

• Silver Cassia *Senna artemisioides*

• Large-flowered Christmas Bell
  Blandfordia grandiflora

Christmas Bushes

 Several States have a plant that is known as Christmas Bush, but the only thing that these plants have in common is that they flower at Christmas time. They have no botanical relationship. Western Australia's Christmas Bush, a beautiful yellow-flowered shrub or tree, is very difficult to cultivate and so is not included.

New South Wales Christmas Bush •
Ceratopetalum gummiferum   Zones: A B C D G

This popular plant comes in several named varieties. The best known is 'Albery's Red', which has excellent deep red colour. This species actually flowers in October–November with small cream flowers; the calyx of the spent flower enlarges and becomes red in December, later in cooler climates. At this stage the calyces are very good for cutting. Reasonably drained sandy soils in full sun suit this plant best. It will reach 5 m in height but can be pruned to keep it smaller. Propagate from seed or cuttings. It is frost hardy. New South Wales Christmas Bush is grown commercially as a cut flower and is an important export earner for Australia. It is sold in Japan as Festival Bush. Many varieties have been developed to extend the flowering season, colour of flower and number of flowers on a stem.

Victorian Christmas Bush • *Prostanthera lasianthos*   Zones: A B C G

This shrub belongs to the group of plants known as mint bushes, a reference to their pleasantly aromatic foliage. It varies in height from 2 m to 10 m and in flower colour from white through pink to mauve, depending on the form. Look carefully at the nursery label before buying. Flowers are borne in large sprays at the end of branches. It will accept most soils and heavy shade. Frost hardy. Propagate from cuttings.

Tasmanian Christmas Bush • *Bursaria spinosa*   *All Zones*

Although flowering at different times in other States, in Tasmania this plant is at its best at Christmas time. It is a prickly shrub to about 3 m with masses of fragrant white flowers borne at the ends of the stems. These are followed by brown fruits that may be used in floral arrangements. It is very hardy in almost all soils and prefers full sun. Propagate from seed or cuttings. It is susceptible to scale, which may be controlled by spraying with white oil. Frost hardy.

• New South Wales Christmas Bush *Ceratopetalum gummiferum*

• Victorian Christmas Bush *Prostanthera lasianthos*   • Tasmanian Christmas Bush *Bursaria spinosa*

Climbers

 Plants climb in several different ways. Some, such as clematis, use their leaf stalks to wind around other plants; many twine their stems; passionfruits and grapes produce climbing organs called tendrils, which are very specialised leaves, and some, like hoyas, produce small roots from their stems to cling onto tree trunks. It is important to understand how a climber functions so that you can decide what type of support it requires. The first three types require wire or mesh to which they can attach themselves. The root climbers, on the other hand, require a rough surface such as a tree trunk with permanent bark or a brick wall that does not require painting. Climbers have many garden uses. They may cover unsightly fences or screen ugly structures. They may even be used as ground covers on banks when trees or shrubs are absent. Several are ideal for covering pergolas.

Painted Billardiera · *Billardiera bicolor*
Zones: A B C G H

This stem climber tends to form a shrub-like mass with its stems twining around each other. It can be trained on a wire frame to about 2 m high. It will perform in most well-drained soils. The green leaves are greyish on the underside. The flowers, cream striped with violet, are about 2.5 cm in diameter and appear in summer and autumn. Propagate from seed. Frost hardy.

Red Billardiera · *Billardiera erubescens*
Zones: A B C G H

This is another stem climber, which will reach 3–4 m on a wire frame. The leaves are bright green and the showy spring flowers are red, about 2.5 cm in diameter and tubular. Most soils are suitable, and the plant is frost hardy and will grow in full sun or part shade. Propagate from seed.

Climbing Flame Pea · *Chorizema diversifolium*
Zones: A B C G

A delicate stem climber with orange-red pea flowers in spring, this plant is best grown in semi- or full shade. It is never dense in habit but the flowers are attractive. Prefers a well-mulched soil with good drainage. Slightly frost tender. Propagate from seed which has been treated with boiling water.

Native Grape or Kangaroo Vine · *Cissus antarctica*
Zones: A B D E

This vigorous rainforest climber uses tendrils to attach itself to a frame or surrounding vegetation. The flowers are insignificant but the attractive foliage is dark green and shiny with toothed margins. The fruits are like small grapes in appearance and are edible. A well-composted soil with some shade is recommended. Grow from cuttings. This species is sometimes used as an indoor plant when young.

• Red Billardiera *Billardiera erubescens*

• Painted Billardiera *Billardiera bicolor*

• Climbing Flame Pea *Chorizema diversifolium*

• Native Grape or Kangaroo Vine *Cissus antarctica*

Traveller's Joy or Old Man's Beard · *Clematis aristata*   *All Zones*

A vigorous climber that uses its leaf stalks to attach itself to a frame or other plants, Traveller's Joy has toothed divided leaves. Its creamy white flowers are borne prolifically in spring, covering the plant, and are followed by a display of feathery fruits. All soils apart from those that are very wet are suitable, in full sun or part shade. Frost hardy. Propagate from cuttings.

Native Lilac · *Hardenbergia comptoniana*   *Zones:* A B C G

Native Lilac is a moderately vigorous stem climber from Western Australia, with shiny three-part leaves and mauve-purple pea flowers in spring. Good drainage and half sun suit this very showy plant best. Frost hardy. Propagate from seed soaked in boiling water overnight.

False Sarsaparilla · *Hardenbergia violacea*   *Zones:* A B C D G

Several cultivars of this very variable species are available from nurseries. 'Happy Wanderer' is a moderately vigorous stem climber producing purple pea flowers from late winter to spring. 'Mini Ha-Ha' is a small plant that is more or less shrub-like, growing only about 50 cm high. Other forms may have pink or white flowers. All are hardy and prefer a sunny position in all but very wet soils. Propagate cultivars from cuttings.

Climbing Guinea Flower · *Hibbertia scandens*   *Zones:* A B D E F G

This moderately vigorous stem climber has large bright green leaves and produces open yellow flowers, about 6 cm in diameter, that are seen for much of the year. They are followed by red fruits that add to the beauty of the plant. It will grow in full sun or part shade in well-drained soil and is resistant to salt spray. Propagate from cuttings.

Common Waxflower · *Hoya australis*   *Zones:* B D E F

All hoyas are slender root climbers. The Common Waxflower is probably the best known of the six native species. It should be grown in part shade or full sun and provided with a tree trunk or wall to grow on. Use a well-composted soil but do not overwater. Its waxy white flowers are fragrant and borne in sprays of 12–40 blooms in summer. Frost tender. Propagate from cuttings.

Native Jasmine · *Jasminum simplicifolium*   *Zones:* B D E F
ssp. *australiense*

Native Jasmine shows some tendency to twine, but mostly its long slender stems just lean on surrounding plants. The leaves are a shiny bright green, and its strongly fragrant white winter flowers have from five to eight petals. Grow in a well-composted soil in full sun. Propagate from seed or cuttings. It may be affected by heavy frosts.

• Native Lilac *Hardenbergia comptoniana*

• Traveller's Joy or Old Man's Beard *Clematis aristata*

• False Sarsaparilla *Hardenbergia violacea*

• Common Waxflower *Hoya australis*

• Climbing Guinea Flower *Hibbertia scandens*

• Native Jasmine *Jasminum simplicifolium* ssp. *australiense*

Black Coral Pea • *Kennedia nigricans*   *Zones:* A B C G

This very vigorous stem climber or ground cover has very large three-part leaves and unusual black and yellow pea flowers in spring. Although recommended for Zone B, it may need protection from heavy frosts. Its stems will spread many metres so space is required. Good drainage and full or part sun give best results. Propagate from seed that has been soaked overnight in boiling water.

Dusky Coral Pea • *Kennedia rubicunda*   *Zones:* A B C D G

This vigorous stem climber will climb to several metres. It may also be used as a ground cover. Red pea flowers are borne in spring. Most soils are suitable, and it will grow in full sun or part shade. Propagate from seed which has been soaked overnight in boiling water.

Bower of Beauty • *Pandorea jasminoides*   *Zones:* A B D E F G

This vigorous stem climber has shiny green foliage and in spring and summer produces large trumpet-shaped flowers that range from pale to dark pink or even white, with a maroon centre. An all-white form is known as 'Lady Di'. It is an excellent plant for covering a trellis or pergola, and prefers well-composted soil in full sun. Slightly frost tender. Propagate from cuttings.

Wonga-wonga Vine • *Pandorea pandorana*   *All Zones*

A hardy and vigorous stem climber, Wonga-wonga Vine gives an attractive display of 2 cm wide tubular flowers in spring. Flower colour varies; 'Golden Showers' is yellow and brown, 'Snow Bells' is white; it is more commonly seen with white and maroon flowers. Most soils are suitable and full sun gives the best flowering. Propagate from cuttings.

Native Passionfruit • *Passiflora cinnabarina*   *Zones:* A B C D G

Like all passionfruits, this species is a tendril climber. It is vigorous and requires a reasonably well-drained soil in full sun or part shade. It has 3-lobed leaves and complex red flowers, to 7 cm in diameter, appearing from spring to summer. While the green fruits are edible they are not very palatable. Propagate from fresh seed or cuttings.

Native Philodendron • *Rhaphidophora australasica*   *Zones:* D E F

Very similar to the exotic philodendrons, this Australian species is suitable for growing outside in warm climates. It may be used as an indoor plant in temperate areas. It is a moderately vigorous root climber and requires a tree trunk or, if used indoors, a tree fern or fibre climbing pole. The large elliptical leaves are up to 40 cm long. The cream summer flowers are rather like those of an arum lily. Grow in a shady spot where it can climb to several metres, and use a well-composted soil. Propagate from cuttings.

• Black Coral Pea *Kennedia nigricans*

• Dusky Coral Pea *Kennedia rubicunda*

• Bower of Beauty *Pandorea jasminoides*

• Wonga-wonga Vine *Pandorea pandorana*

• Native Passionfruit *Passiflora cinnabarina*

• Native Philodendron *Raphidophora australasica*

Bluebell Creeper · *Sollya heterophylla* Zones: A B C D G

Blue is not a common colour amongst Australian flowers but this stem climber bears a profusion of light blue bell flowers in spring and summer. It is very hardy, quite vigorous and will accept most soils and aspects. As birds are attracted to the seeds, take care that the plant does not escape into local bush. Remove the seeds if it is to be grown near bushland. Propagate from seed or cuttings.

Fraser Island Creeper · *Tecomanthe hillii* Zones: B D E

There are few more attractive climbers for warm areas than this stem climber, native to Fraser Island in Queensland, which will reach 4–5 m high. The pinkish red bell-shaped flowers, carried on the old wood, are about 10 cm long and appear in late spring or summer. They are much favoured by nectar-seeking birds. Grow in a well-composted soil in a morning sun position. Propagate from cuttings.

Conesticks and Drumsticks

*Conesticks (*Petrophile*) and drumsticks (*Isopogon*) belong to the family Proteaceae, along with with banksias and grevilleas. The common names are derived from the shape of their seedheads, which in the case of conesticks comprise a series of overlapping plates each covering a seed and forming a cone-like shape rather like a pine cone. Drumsticks form a similarly structured seedhead, but it is rather more globular in shape, resembling a drumstick. Many of the more attractive species are natural to Western Australia and are difficult to grow on the humid east coast and in the tropics. However, several east coast species are also worthwhile and are included here. All these plants require excellent drainage and most prefer full sun. They may be propagated from the feathery seeds, which are released when the head is mature and dried.*

Granite Conesticks · *Petrophile biloba* Zones: A G

Growing to 2 m high, this open shrub from Western Australia is improved in form by regular pruning. The lobed leaves are sharply pointed and the pink woolly flowers are borne in the leaf junctions in spring. The cones of this species are very small. It is an excellent shrub for winter rainfall areas.

Grey Conesticks · *Petrophile canescens* Zones: A B C D G

This tiny east coast shrub usually reaches only about 70 cm high. Its much-divided greyish leaves are an attractive garden feature. In spring and summer creamy yellow flowers about 2 cm in diameter appear at the ends of the branches or in the leaf junctions. It will grow in most soils and is frost hardy.

• Bluebell Creeper *Sollya heterophylla*

• Fraser Island Creeper *Tecomanthe hillii*

• Granite Conesticks *Petrophile biloba*

• Grey Conesticks *Petrophile canescens*

Drumsticks • *Isopogon anemonifolius*   Zones: A B C D G H
A hardy shrub to 2 m high by 1.5 m across, this species has light green much-divided leaves with flattened lobes. The large yellow globular flowerheads are prominently displayed in spring. Good drainage and full to part sun are recommended. Frost hardy.

Fine-leaved Drumsticks • *Isopogon anethifolius*   Zones: A B C D G H
A very handsome shrub to 2 m high by 2 m across, this species has dainty, finely divided leaves and reddish stems, particularly on the young growth. The large yellow globular flowerheads are prominently displayed in spring. It will grow in most reasonably drained soils in full to part sun. Frost hardy. It may be used as a cut flower.

Pincushion Coneflower • *Isopogon dubius*   Zones: A G H
This small erect shrub rarely exceeds 60 cm in height. It has divided leaves with prickly tips and pink globular flowerheads borne on the tips of the branchlets in spring. Excellent drainage is essential. Frost hardy.

Broad-leaved Drumsticks • *Isopogon latifolius*   Zones: A G
This beautiful plant is grown commercially as a cut flower in areas of winter rainfall but is extremely difficult to grow on the east coast. It reaches 2 m high by 1.5 m across, with elliptical leaves up to 10 cm long. Large pink terminal flowers, about 6 cm in diameter, appear in spring and are followed by globular cones to about 4.5 cm in diameter.

Correas

There are 11 species of Correa *in Australia and all but one occur naturally in the south-eastern States. The other is found just across the border in southern Western Australia. Correas are hardy shrubs for temperate areas. They vary in form from prostrate to plants more than 3 m high. Their bell-shaped flowers may be white, pink, red, green or red and yellow. The foliage is neat and the flowers attract birds. Good drainage is important. All species are frost hardy and all will accept some shade and still flower well.*

Spreading Correa • *Correa decumbens*   Zones: A B C G
This low, spreading plant will cover an area about 1.5 m across and about 30 cm high in the centre of the plant. The foliage is dark green and the red and yellow-green tubular flowers are held erect. The flowers appear in winter. This species makes a useful ground cover for temperate areas. Propagate from cuttings.

• **Drumsticks** *Isopogon anemonifolius*

• **Fine-leaved Drumsticks** *Isopogon anethifolius*

• **Pincushion Coneflower** *Isopogon dubius*

• **Broad-leaved Drumsticks** *Isopogon latifolius*

• **Spreading Correa** *Correa decumbens*

Dusky Bells · *Correa 'Dusky Bells'*   *Zones:* **A** B C **G**

This cultivar is a hybrid between *Correa reflexa* and *C. pulchella*, a spreading shrub to 80 cm high and up to 3 m across. The pendent bell flowers, carmine-pink and about 4 cm long, appear from autumn to early spring. It prefers part shade in most well-drained soils. Propagate from cuttings. *Correa 'Mannii'* is similar but generally larger, with darker flowers.

Tiny Correa · *Correa pulchella*   *Zones:* **A** B C **G**

A dainty shrub with light green leaves, rarely exceeding 50 cm in height, this correa produces orange to pink bell-shaped flowers in winter. It makes an excellent pot plant for a half sun position or may be grown in a rockery. Propagate from cuttings.

Common Correa · *Correa reflexa*   *Zones:* **A** B C **G**

This species is very variable in habit, flower colour and flower shape, but most forms are worth growing. A form from the central coast of New South Wales, and another from South Australia, are the most attractive. They are compact plants to 50 cm high by 50 cm across and produce broad red bells with a yellow-green tip in winter. Taller plants from the southern tablelands of New South Wales often have green flowers and form a straggly bush. Good drainage is very important. Propagate from cuttings.

Daisies

 Daisies comprise one of the largest plant families in the world, with over 25 000 species. Australia has about 1000 species, many of which are worth growing in your garden. They may be annuals (refer to page 12), small rockery plants or woody shrubs. Most are hardy and do well in sunny positions in reasonably well-drained soils. Pruning is usually important for the shrubby species as they can become leggy with unsightly dead leaves at the base. Prune lightly after flowering.

ROCKERY PLANTS

Cut-leaf Daisy · *Brachyscome multifida*   *Zones:* **A** B C **D** E **G H**

This well-known little plant varies in flower colour from white through pinks to blue and mauve, with yellow centres. It forms a rounded plant about 30 cm across by 30 cm high with bright green divided leaves. Flowers are present for most of the year. Full sun is best for good flowering. Frost hardy. It may occasionally self-seed in the garden but never becomes a pest. Propagate from cuttings, which root readily.

• **Dusky Bells** *Correa* 'Dusky Bells' • **Tiny Correa** *Correa pulchella*

• **Common Correa** *Correa reflexa* • **Cut-leaf Daisy** *Brachyscome multifida*

Sunburst · *Brachyscome 'Sunburst'*   *Zones:* A B C D E G H

While this plant is similar in habit to the Cut-leaf Daisy, its flowers open a deep apricot and age to fawn, cream and mauve, giving a multi-coloured effect. It makes a good basket plant and has the same cultivation requirements as Cut-Leaf Daisy. Frost hardy.

Pilliga Daisy · *Brachyscome formosa*   *Zones:* A B C D G H

This small suckering perennial will reach 15 cm high and spread to 40 cm. The flowers are mauve, about 2 cm in diameter, and appear in spring and summer. It is ideal as a rockery plant, requiring good drainage and withstanding dry periods. Frost hardy. Propagate by division or from cuttings.

Paper Cascade · *Rhodanthe anthemoides*   *Zones:* A B C

A rounded plant about 50 cm high by 30 cm across, this small perennial has greyish foliage and produces masses of 2 cm diameter papery white flowers with yellow centres in late spring and summer. Cut back after flowering to encourage new shoots, which will bear the next season's flowers. Good drainage and full sun are recommended. Frost hardy. Propagate from cuttings.

Billy Buttons · *Pycnosorus globosus*   *Zones:* A B C G H

Forming a rosette of woolly, silvery leaves about 40 cm in diameter, this perennial produces an erect flowering stem to 80 cm high with a globular golden yellow flowerhead, quite unlike a typical daisy flower in appearance. The spring and summer flowers are excellent cut flowers and were used in the presentation bouquets at the Sydney 2000 Olympic Games. Very good drainage is important. It will grow in full sun and is frost hardy. Propagate from seed.

Diamond Head · *Bracteantha 'Diamond Head'*   *Zones:* A B C D G H

This everlasting daisy is a perennial found naturally on headlands of the mid-north coast of New South Wales. It forms a compact plant about 30 cm high by 60 cm across. The papery flowers are bright golden yellow and borne on stems to 15 cm long in summer and autumn. After flowering the stems should be cut back to make room for new growth. Most soils are suitable but grow in full sun. It is frost hardy and resistant to salt spray.

• **Pilliga Daisy** *Brachyscome formosa*

• **Sunburst** *Brachyscome* 'Sunburst'

• **Paper Cascade** *Rhodanthe anthemoides*

• **Billy Buttons** *Pycnosorus globosus*

• **Diamond Head** *Bracteantha* 'Diamond Head'

SHRUBS

Daisy Bush • *Olearia phlogopappa*
Zones: A B C

The genus *Olearia* has many species but this is probably the best. It has been cultivated in Europe and the UK for many years and several colour forms are available. It forms a shrub to 1.5 m high by 1 m across with grey-green leaves. Most naturally occurring plants have white flowers but special selections have been made with blue, pink or mauve flowers. These are very good garden plants which are resistant to heavy frosts. Full sun and good drainage are required. Propagate from cuttings.

Rice Flower • *Ozothamnus diosmifolius*
Zones: A B C D G H

Grown commercially as an export crop, this plant is excellent for cut flowers. It forms a shrub about 2.5 m high by 2 m across. The tiny white or, rarely, pink flowers are borne in terminal sprays in late spring and summer. Pruning after flowering helps to shape the plant. It is hardy in most soils but flowers best in full sun. Frost hardy. Grow from cuttings.

Yellow Rice Flower • *Ozothamnus obcordatus*
Zones: A B C D G

A small shrub to about 1.5 m, in spring this plant produces large heads of tiny yellow flowers, each about 5 mm in diameter. The leaves are dark green on top and grey on the underside. It is hardy in most soils and will tolerate some shade. Prune after flowering to maintain a good shape. Frost hardy. Propagate from cuttings of new growth which has begun to harden.

Dog Rose

 Dog Rose belongs to the small genus Bauera, *which has one species in the Grampians of Victoria, one on the coastal heaths of northern New South Wales and southern Queensland and the other, more widespread, occurring from southern Queensland to Tasmania and Kangaroo Island. It is this last species that has proved the hardiest in cultivation and is highly recommended for garden use.*

Dog Rose or River Rose • *Bauera rubioides*
Zones: A B C D G

This is a wonderful shrub for temperate or subtropical gardens. The common form grows into a dense bush 1.5 m high by 2 m across with masses of pink flowers in spring and early summer. The individual flowers look like tiny single roses and tend to face downwards. It will grow in most soils, even accepting quite damp situations. In shade the shrub becomes taller with long straggly branches, but in part sun or full sun it is much more compact. Tip pruning is advisable after flowering. A white form is often available. The dwarf form *Bauera rubioides* var. *microphylla* is smaller in all its parts and is suitable for rockery use. All forms are frost hardy.

• Daisy Bush *Olearia phlogopappa*

• Rice Flower *Ozothamnus diosmifolius*

• Yellow Rice Flower *Ozothamnus obcordatus*

• Dog Rose or River Rose *Bauera rubioides*

Emu Bushes or Poverty Bushes

These strangely named plants are members of the genus Eremophila, *which means 'desert-loving'. There are 217 species in the genus, all native to Australia, with one also occurring in New Zealand. They are found in semi-arid areas where the climate is harsh and plant variety is generally limited, hence the name 'poverty bush'. The seeds are very hard and it is said that they have to pass through an emu's digestive system before they will germinate, giving rise to their other common name. These plants have beautiful flowers in many different colours and make excellent garden subjects in suitable climates.*

Red Rod · *Eremophila calorhabdos*   *Zones:* **A** G **H**
This erect, sparsely branched shrub will reach 2 m with crowded 2 cm leaves surrounding the stems. The 3 cm tubular flowers are magenta and borne in the leaf axils towards the end of branches in spring and summer. It needs excellent drainage in full sun, with some air movement to reduce the chance of fungal infection in humid weather. Prune regularly to encourage branching. Frost hardy. Propagate from cuttings.

Amulla · *Eremophila debilis*   *Zones:* **A B** C **G H**
Until recently this species was known as a *Myoporum* and may still be sold in nurseries as such. It is a prostrate ground cover which will cover a circle of about 50 cm diameter. It produces small white or pale lilac flowers in the leaf axils in spring, followed by globular red, purple or green edible fruits about 1 cm in diameter. It is also suitable for growing in baskets. Sun or part shade and good drainage are required. This species is slightly frost tender. Propagate from cuttings.

Spotted Emu Bush · *Eremophila maculata*   *Zones:* **A B** C **G H**
Probably the most common species of *Eremophila* in cultivation, and one of the most showy, this plant is very variable in flower colour. It usually forms a rounded shrub up to 2 m high by 2 m across with tubular flowers to 2.5 cm long in the upper leaf axils in spring. They are borne on long s-shaped stalks to 2.5 cm long. Most often spotted, their colour may be yellow, pink, mauve or red. This is a very hardy plant given well-drained soil and a sunny site. Frost hardy. Propagate from cuttings.

Grey-leaved Emu Bush · *Eremophila nivea*   *Zones:* **A B** C **G H**
This beautiful shrub is being grown commercially as a cut flower in southern New South Wales, and may be grafted onto hardy rootstock to increase its adaptability over a wider range of climates. It grows to about 2 m high by 1.5 m across and has silvery grey foliage, which contrasts well with the purple tubular spring flowers. Grafted plants are sometimes available from nurseries. Well-drained soils in full sun are recommended. Frost hardy.

• Red Rod *Eremophila calorhabdos*

• **Amulla** *Eremophila debilis*

• Spotted Emu Bush *Eremophila maculata*

• Grey-leaved Emu Bush *Eremophila nivea*

Eucalypts

 With well over 700 species, this large genus typifies the Australian bush. Many are too large for a small garden and a selection of medium- or small-growing species is given here. While eucalypts occur over most of the country, you must take care to select species that are suitable for your climate. If you do this you will find them easy and reliable additions to your garden. Some eucalypts are grown for their flowers, which may be cream, pink or red, and others are grown for their form, offering shade and shelter. A selection of both types is given below. Some botanists place eucalypts in several genera and the alternative generic name is shown in brackets.

Silver Princess · *Eucalyptus caesia* ssp. *magna*   *Zones:* A C G H

This slender tree may reach about 10 m in height with an open habit and beautiful pendulous branches bearing large reddish pink flowers in spring. The smaller branches and flower stalks are covered with a white bloom, which gives the tree a silvery appearance. The large bell-shaped fruits have the same white covering. The reddish brown bark of the trunk peels in summer to reveal the new green bark. It should be used as a feature plant in climates with a dry summer. Full sun and good drainage are required and it is frost hardy. Propagate from seed.

Argyle Apple · *Eucalyptus cinerea*   *Zones:* A C

This is an excellent shade tree for cool and cold climates. It has silvery grey rounded juvenile leaves which change to the typical eucalypt shape as the plant ages. The adult leaves are also silvery grey. The bark is stringy and the tree produces a shady crown to 12 m in height by 15 m diameter. The cream flowers are produced in late spring and summer. Most soils are suitable. Frost hardy. Propagate from seed. Occasionally leaf-eating caterpillars may damage the foliage but the tree will recover.

Lemon-scented Gum · *Eucalyptus (Corymbia) citriodora*   *Zones:* B D E G

This tall, slender, smooth-barked gum, which can reach 25 m in height, may be a little large for a small suburban garden but makes a fine feature tree for the larger property. The foliage has a strong citrus perfume. The small winter flowers are cream. Hardy in frost-free areas. Propagate from seed.

Plunkett Mallee · *Eucalyptus curtisii*   *Zones:* A B C D E

Often developing a multi-trunked habit, this small tree to 6 m high, often less, is suitable for even the smallest garden. It has smooth greenish grey bark and masses of cream flowers in late spring and summer. A well-drained sunny site is recommended. Frost hardy. Propagate from seed.

• Silver Princess *Eucalyptus caesia* ssp. *magna*   • Argyle Apple *Eucalyptus cinerea*

• Lemon-scented Gum *Eucalyptus*   • Plunkett Mallee *Eucalyptus curtisii*
(Corymbia) citriodora

Fuchsia Gum · *Eucalyptus forrestiana*   *Zones:* A G H

This small bushy tree rarely exceeds 5 m high by 3 m across. Its four-angled pendulous buds, and the fruits, are bright red while the spring flowers are yellow, giving the tree an extended period of beauty. Good drainage is advisable. Prefers a sunny site. Slightly frost tender. Propagate from seed.

Scribbly Gum · *Eucalyptus haemastoma*   *Zones:* A B C D G

So named for the scribble-like markings on its cream bark, this small tree usually forms a crooked trunk and is ideal for an informal garden. The markings are formed by the larvae of a moth which move about beneath the bark; the movements are apparent as scribbles when the bark is shed. The tree reaches about 10 m in height and its crown creates light shade. The small cream flowers may appear in various seasons. Prefers well-drained sandy soil and most aspects are suitable. Propagate from seed.

Narrow-leaved Peppermint · *Eucalyptus nicholii*   *Zones:* A B C

Although very popular, this handsome well-shaped tree will reach 15 m in height and may crowd a small garden. It has fibrous brown bark and its narrow leaves are grey-green, forming a dense canopy. The cream autumn flowers are insignificant. Most soils and aspects are suitable. Propagate from seed.

Scarlet Gum · *Eucalyptus phoenicea*   *Zones:* E F

Reaching 10 m in height, Scarlet Gum is a wonderful tree for tropical gardens. Its bark is flaky, brown and cream and its leaves are light green, forming an open canopy. The large bunches of orange to scarlet flowers appearing in various months are a feature and their nectar attracts birds. This tree is best grown in a sunny position in well-drained soil. Propagate from seed.

Swamp Bloodwood · *Eucalyptus (Corymbia) ptychocarpa*   *Zones:* D E F

A most attractive tree for tropical and subtropical gardens, Swamp Bloodwood adapts to most soils and aspects. The 4 cm diameter flowers, borne in large bunches, may be red, pink or white and are seen sporadically but more frequently in winter in subtropical climates. They are followed by a large urn-shaped fruit. The leaves are very large, sometimes up to 30 cm long. Frost tender. Propagate from seed, although the progeny may not come true to colour.

Summer Beauty · *Eucalyptus (Corymbia)* 'Summer Beauty'   *Zones:* D E F G

Summer Beauty is a hybrid between the Western Australian *Eucalyptus ficifolia* and the tropical *E. ptychocarpa*. Although relatively new in cultivation, it is proving hardy and gives a great display of large pink flowers several times during the year. As it is a grafted plant, it is usually a little more expensive to buy. Most soils are suitable. 'Summer Red' is similar but has red flowers.

• Fuchsia Gum *Eucalyptus forrestiana*

• Scribbly Gum *Eucalyptus haemastoma*

• Narrow-leaved Peppermint *Eucalyptus nicholii*

• Scarlet Gum *Eucalyptus phoenicea*

• Swamp Bloodwood *Eucalyptus (Corymbia) ptychocarpa*

• Summer Beauty *Eucalyptus (Corymbia)* 'Summer Beauty'

Tallerack · *Eucalyptus pleurocarpa*   Zones: A C G H

This usually multi-stemmed shrub forms a large bushy plant to 4 m high by about 5 m across. It has silvery grey leaves, white stems, buds and fruits, and cream flowers in late spring and early summer. The squarish gumnuts are popular in floral arrangements. Good drainage and a sunny position are essential. Frost hardy. Propagate from seed.

Coral Gum · *Eucalyptus torquata*   Zones: A C G H

This small, spreading tree to 8 m in height, used as a street tree in dry areas, bears masses of pink flowers in spring and summer. The buds and fruits are ribbed and reddish in colour. Full sun and a well-drained soil are recommended. Frost hardy. Propagate from seed.

Fan Flowers and Their Relatives

With few exceptions, the plants in the family Goodeniaceae, to which the fan flowers belong, are unique to Australia. They are mainly small colourful plants suitable for rockeries, baskets or pots. Almost all require excellent drainage and grow best in full to half sun.

Mat Dampiera · *Dampiera diversifolia*   Zones: A C G

This prostrate plant suckers and spreads to about 50 cm across, making a dense ground cover. Its small mid-green leaves, up to 3 cm long, are often bunched together. The dark blue flowers cover the plant in spring and summer. It will grow well in a hanging basket or in a well-drained rockery pocket. Frost hardy. Propagate from cuttings.

Common Dampiera · *Dampiera stricta*   Zones: A B C D

Like Mat Dampiera, this is a suckering plant, but its stems may reach 40 cm in height and its growth habit is much less dense. The leaves are borne on semi-erect stems and the flowers, varying from light to dark blue, have a yellow centre. They appear mainly in spring and summer. Most soils and aspects are suitable. Propagate from cuttings or by division.

Forest Goodenia · *Goodenia hederacea*   Zones: A B C D

Occasionally rooting at the nodes, this trailing plant is a delight in the rockery. With dark green, mostly toothed leaves and yellow flowers in spring and summer, its dense habit makes it a good ground cover or basket plant. It is hardy in most soils and will accept some shade. Frost hardy. Propagate from cuttings.

• Tallerack *Eucalyptus pleurocarpa*

• **Coral Gum** *Eucalyptus torquata*

• **Mat Dampiera** *Dampiera diversifolia*

• **Forest Goodenia** *Goodenia hederacea*

• **Common Dampiera** *Dampiera stricta*

Hop Goodenia • *Goodenia ovata*   *Zones:* **A** B C D

More shrub-like than most other species of *Goodenia*, the quick-growing Hop Goodenia will grow to 1.5 m high by 60 cm across and should be regularly pruned to maintain a reasonable shape. It is a very adaptable species, accepting full shade to full sun, and wet to well-drained soils. The yellow flowers appear in spring and summer. Frost hardy. Propagate from cuttings.

Blue Lechenaultia • *Lechenaultia biloba*   *Zones:* **A** G

Producing the most vividly blue flower in the Australian flora, this small plant is not easy to maintain on the east coast unless it is grown in a container where drainage can be controlled. In less humid areas it may be grown in a rockery, in full or part sun. Plants reach about 50 cm in height with soft, almost succulent, grey-green leaves. The flowers, which vary from white through to the most beautiful deep blue, appear in spring. It is moderately frost hardy. As this species may be grown very easily from cuttings, it is well worth taking cuttings each year.

Red Lechenaultia • *Lechenaultia formosa*   *Zones:* **A** G

Like Blue Lechenaultia, this prostrate or semi-erect plant is also difficult to maintain on the east coast unless it is grown in a container or basket. Flower colour varies from white through yellow, red and rose to scarlet, and combinations of these colours. It is spring flowering, and an excellent rockery plant for areas with dry summers. It is moderately frost hardy. It is easy to grow from cuttings.

Fan Flower • *Scaevola aemula*   *Zones:* **A** B D G H

This prostrate plant varies in both flower size and vigour. Some selected forms are available commercially. The fan-shaped flowers are mauve-blue and in good forms are borne prolifically in spring and summer. It is an excellent plant for rockeries, where its trailing stems may reach 50 cm long. Good drainage and full to part sun are best. Slightly frost tender. Propagate from cuttings.

Small Fan Flower • *Scaevola albida*   *Zones:* **A** B C D G H

Similar to *Scaevola aemula* but smaller in all its parts, this prostrate plant will spread to about 50 cm across. Flower colour varies from white to light blue; flowering continues for many months from early spring. Reasonable drainage and full to part sun are recommended. It is a reliable rockery plant. Propagate from cuttings. Frost hardy.

• Hop Goodenia *Goodenia ovata*

• Red Lechenaultia *Lechenaultia formosa*

• Blue Lechenaultia *Lechenaultia biloba*

• Fan Flower *Scaevola aemula*

• Small Fan Flower *Scaevola albida*

Feather Flowers

 Feather flowers belong to the genus Verticordia *and are so named because their sepals are much divided, giving a feathery, intricate appearance to the flowers. There are over 100 species in the genus and almost without exception they have great horticultural appeal. Unfortunately, however, most have proved difficult to propagate and cultivate. The two species mentioned below are hardy in areas where the summers have low humidity and light rainfall. Excellent drainage in a sunny situation suits them best. Both may be grown in containers where watering may be more easily controlled.*

Yellow Feather Flower · *Verticordia chrysantha*   *Zones:* **A G H**

An erect shrub to 60 cm high by 50 cm across, Yellow Feather Flower has light green linear leaves and masses of bright yellow feathery flowers in spring. The flowers cover the plant and are excellent for cutting. It is a good container plant. Frost hardy. Propagate from cuttings taken after flowering has finished and new growth has begun to harden.

Plumed Feather Flower · *Verticordia plumosa*   *Zones:* **A G H**

Foliage on this variable species is generally grey-green and the fluffy spring flowers are mostly pink. Plants may reach 50 cm as a rounded shrub, but taller forms are also known. It is a good container plant and probably the hardiest member of the genus. Frost hardy. Propagate from cuttings taken when new growth hardens after flowering.

Ferns

 There are more than 400 species of ferns in the Australian flora, varying from the tiny filmy ferns of the moist rainforests to the tall stately tree ferns of east Gippsland and the huge bird's nest ferns nestling high on rainforest trees. In general, ferns prefer a shady situation with ample moisture available in dry seasons. Many make attractive pot plants that may be brought indoors for short periods. Ferns grow best in a rich loamy soil with plenty of organic matter, and a good mulch of leaf mould or compost to help retain soil moisture and keep the root run cool. Most ferns are relatively pest-free in the wild, but mealy bugs and white fly can cause damage in a fernery. These can be controlled with the appropriate sprays, such as white oil mixed with an insecticide. Be careful when spraying young fronds as they may be burned by full-strength applications. Most ferns will not tolerate heavy frosts. Propagation of most ferns is not easy and is generally best left to fern specialists.

• Yellow Feather Flower *Verticordia chrysantha*

• Plumed Feather Flower *Verticordia plumosa*

Common Maiden Hair Fern · *Adiantum aethiopicum*   *Zones:* A B D E G

The lacy fronds of this popular fern reach 30–50 cm in height on slender glossy black stems. Given shade or part shade and ample moisture, it will produce a lovely plant. A good garden subject, it also makes a good potted specimen or basket plant to bring indoors for short periods.

Mother Spleenwort or Hen and Chickens Fern ·
Asplenium bulbiferum   *Zones:* A B D E G

More robust than Maiden Hair Fern, this is a clumping plant with much-divided fronds up to 1 m long. New plants may be produced by carefully removing the tiny plantlets produced on the tips of the fronds and planting them in a new pot. The young plants should be kept in a humid atmosphere in a potting mix that includes peat moss. It is hardy in the garden provided some shade and ample moisture are available.

Fishbone Water Fern · *Blechnum nudum*   *Zones:* A B C D E G

There are about 18 species of water fern (members of the genus *Blechnum*) in Australia, and this is one of the hardiest. It is a tufted plant that on aging develops a short fibrous trunk to 30–40 cm. The feathery fronds are up to 70 cm long. Shade and moisture are the keys to success. Spores will germinate in the garden if conditions are favourable.

Rough Tree Fern · *Cyathea australis*   *Zones:* B D E

This is probably the most common tree fern in eastern Australia. The trunk will reach 10 m in height and the spreading fronds, which radiate from the top of the trunk, will reach 4 m in good conditions. High humidity, ample water and some shade are essential for good growth. Young plants may be found germinating in favourable sites in the garden. These can be readily transplanted.

Scaly Tree Fern · *Cyathea cooperi*   *Zones:* B D E

So named for the brown scales that form on the new fronds before they fully expand, the Scaly Tree Fern is the fastest growing of the tree ferns. It forms a trunk up to 12 m in height with fronds to 4 or 5 m long. It is a wonderful specimen plant for humid regions. Treat similarly to Rough Tree Fern.

Soft Tree Fern · *Dicksonia antarctica*   *Zones:* A B C

Growing naturally at higher altitudes than the other species listed here, this plant is more cold tolerant. It is also more robust, with a thicker trunk and slightly slower growth. Its ultimate size, however, is even greater — it can reach 15 m in height in the forests of east Gippsland. As this plant has a network of roots on its trunk, it may be sawn off above the ground and the top transplanted. The piece left behind, however, will die. After transplanting, water should be drizzled over the trunk at regular intervals. Buy from a reputable nursery with a supplier's label attached to the plant — it is illegal to collect from the wild without a licence.

• Common Maiden Hair Fern
Adiantum aethiopicum

• Mother Spleenwort or Hen and Chickens Fern
Asplenium bulbiferum

• Fishbone Water Fern *Blechnum nudum*

• Rough Tree Fern *Cyathea australis*

• Scaly Tree Fern *Cyathea cooperi*

• Soft Tree Fern *Dicksonia antarctica*

Figs

There are about 1000 species of figs distributed around the warm areas of the world. Some are enormous trees; others, like the Mediterranean fig, Ficus carica, *are an important food source. Australia has 42 native species, most of which occur naturally in rainforest and in general are too big for the average garden. Some species, however, are commonly used as indoor plants while they are small.*

Weeping Fig · *Ficus benjamina*
Zones: B D **E** F G

Sometimes used on large properties as an avenue tree, reaching 20 m, this species is far too big for the average garden. It may, however, be used indoors or on a patio in a large container and is hardy even in air-conditioned rooms. The cultivar 'Baby Ben' has been specially selected for this purpose and is generally available from nurseries. Use a commercial potting mix and stand in a position where the plant will receive good light. Water regularly and occasionally move the plant outside to give it a squirt with a hose to remove dust. The foliage is bright green and the branches are slightly pendulous. Never be tempted to plant it out in the garden when you don't want it as a pot plant any more, as the roots are extremely vigorous.

Flannel Flowers

The Sydney Flannel Flower is by far the best known member of the genus Actinotus, *and the only one available in nurseries. It is grown commercially for the cut-flower trade.*

Sydney Flannel Flower · *Actinotus helianthi*
Zones: **A** B D G

The wonderful large daisy-like spring and summer flowers of this plant, with felt-textured 'petals', contrast well with the silvery grey, much-divided foliage. This species, which grows to 50 cm high, requires a sandy soil with excellent drainage and does best with a cool root run. This can be provided by placing slabs of sandstone around the base of the plant or using a good mulch. Full sun gives the best flowering. Sydney Flannel Flower may also be grown in large pots where the drainage and watering regime may be more easily controlled. Cut the flowers for a bushier plant. Slightly frost tender. Propagate from seed, which is often slow to germinate; they do not often self-seed.

• Weeping Fig *Ficus benjamina*

• Sydney Flannel Flower *Actinotus helianthi*

Flax Lilies

Flax lilies belong to the genus Dianella. *About 15 of the 30 known species occur in Australia. Hardy plants suitable for a rockery or border, they all have branching sprays of blue flowers with prominent yellow anthers, followed by bright blue fruits, and provide a long period of interest in the garden. Most soils are suitable and they will accept part shade or full sun. All are frost hardy. Propagation is from seed or by division of rhizomes.*

Paroo Lily · *Dianella caerulea* — *All Zones*

This is one of the taller flax lilies and is very variable in form over its vast natural range. The deep green leaves are 10–60 cm long and the flowers are borne from spring to early summer on branching stems to 90 cm long. Flower colour varies from pale to dark blue, with prominent yellow stamens. The globular berries, about 1 cm in diameter, also vary in colour, from pale blue to deep purple.

Tasman Flax Lily · *Dianella tasmanica* — Zones: **A** B C D

More suited to areas with ample water, this clumping species has short rhizomes and leaves to 80 cm long. In spring the branching flower stem may reach 1.5 m in height; the flowers are blue and are followed by blue fruits up to 2 cm long. Very hardy as long as it is well watered, it will spread to cover an area about a metre square.

Fringe Myrtles

Members of the genus Calytrix *are commonly known as 'fringe myrtles' or 'star flowers'. They occur in all States and some are very colourful. Two species from the 75 that occur in Australia are selected here — one for the tropics and one for milder areas.*

Common Fringe Myrtle · *Calytrix tetragona* — Zones: **A** B C D **G H**

Variable in size and flower colour, this species occurs naturally all over southern Australia and into southern Queensland. It forms a rounded shrub from 30 cm to over 1.5 m high. The heath-like leaves are up to 1.5 cm long and the star-shaped spring flowers, up to 2 cm in diameter, vary from white to deep pink. When the flower falls, the reddish calyx, with its thread-like extensions, remains on the shrub to extend the period of colour. Good drainage is important and full sun to part shade is suitable. Frost hardy. Propagate from cuttings.

• Paroo Lily *Dianella caerulea*

• Tasman Flax Lily *Dianella tasmanica*

• Common Fringe Myrtle *Calytrix tetragona*

Turkey Bush • *Calytrix exstipulata*   *Zones:* **E F H**

Several tropical shrubs seem to have attracted the common name Turkey Bush, apparently because wild turkeys tend to roost in them. This species forms a shrub or small tree to 5 m in height with a furrowed, fibrous trunk. The leaves are small but the vivid pink flowers produced throughout the year are spectacular. Good drainage and full sun or a little shade are recommended. This species is likely to be frost tender. Propagate from cuttings.

Fringed Violets or Fringed Lilies

 The genus Thysanotus *is related to lilies but is now generally placed in the family Anthericaceae. There are 49 species, mostly Australian, with one in South-East Asia and two in Papua New Guinea. They are perennial herbs, often reduced to tubers after flowering. Their flowers are various shades of purple and each flower only lasts one day, opening early in the morning and usually withering by early afternoon. All make suitable rockery plants or container plants for a fernery. They require very good drainage and appreciate a rest period after flowering. Watering should be reduced at this time. Most species flower in spring or early summer. They will accept full sun or a little shade. The Climbing Fringed Violet mentioned below is the only climbing member of the genus.*

Western Fringed Violet • *Thysanotus multiflorus*   *Zones:* **A G H**

This tufted, moderately robust spring-flowering plant has pale green leaves about 30 cm long and pale purple three-petalled flowers to 3 cm in diameter. Several flowers are borne together on the end of a 30 cm stem, each flower fringed with a row of hairs. Excellent drainage is essential, but water only in dry periods. This plant does not do well on the humid east coast. Propagate from seed.

Climbing Fringed Violet • *Thysanotus patersonii*   *Zones:* **A** B C **G H**

A weak stem climber depending on the support of surrounding plants, this plant's leafless stems rarely exceed about 80 cm. Masses of fringed purple flowers are borne along the stems in spring and summer. The plant develops tubers which assist in its survival during dry periods. Frost hardy. Propagate from seed.

• Turkey Bush *Calytrix exstipulata*

• Western Fringed Violet *Thysanotus multiflorus*

• Climbing Fringed Violet *Thysanotus patersonii*

Gingers and Their Relatives

Gingers tend to be mainly tropical plants. If you live in a cooler area they are best treated as glasshouse plants, but in the tropics and subtropics they make excellent garden features. Some are evergreen and others are reduced to underground rhizomes during the dry season.

Native Ginger • *Alpinia caerulea*
Zones: B D E F

With leafy stems reaching 1.5 m, this is an attractive foliage plant for a shady well-watered spot. Plenty of organic matter in the soil will help this rainforest understorey plant feel at home. The small white flowers, seen throughout the year, are borne at the tip of the stem in a spike about 20 cm long and are followed by globular blue fruits, which are enjoyed by the Satin Bower Bird. The rhizome may be eaten and has a distinctive ginger flavour. Frost tender. Propagate by seed or division of rhizome.

Cape York Lily • *Curcuma australasica*
Zones: D E F

Cape York Lily develops its flowers at the beginning of summer (the start of the wet season) and the leaves follow shortly afterwards. The flower spike is about 40 cm high with the yellow flowers nestling inside lolly pink bracts which fade to green as the flower ages. The spade-shaped leaves are about 60 cm long. The flower spike makes a spectacular cut flower. This plant does well in the garden but requires at least half sun to flower well. It should be kept reasonably dry in the dormant (winter) season. Frost tender. Propagate from seed, which is slow to germinate, or by division.

Grass Trees

Grass trees belong to the genus Xanthorrhoea *which is endemic to Australia and includes some 28 species. Grass trees are slow growing and may live to a great age. Some species are apparently trunkless but actually develop a thickened underground stem. Others develop a thick trunk that may reach several metres in height with a tuft of deep green stiff leaves at the top. In the wild the trunk is often exposed, blackened by fire, but in cultivation remains covered by a 'skirt' of old leaves. The flower spike towers above the plant, a long shaft up to 2 m in length with cream flowers covering the top half. The unique form of these plants makes them suitable for use as a feature in a garden. Mature or semi-mature plants may be purchased from reputable nurseries — but ensure that the plants have been established in their containers for some months and are not just recently transplanted from the wild, as relocation is not always successful.*

• Native Ginger *Alpinia caerulea*

• Cape York Lily *Curcuma australasica*

Common Grass Tree · *Xanthorrhoea australis*   *Zones:* Ⓐ Ⓑ C Ⓓ Ⓖ

This species develops a trunk as it ages but this may take many years. It has been recorded in cultivation as producing its first flower spike in as little as six years from seed. The long grass-like leaves will reach 1 m in length and flowers are usually formed in spring and early summer. Good drainage is important. Frost hardy. Propagate from seed.

Dwarf Grass Tree · *Xanthorrhoea macronema*   *Zones:* Ⓐ Ⓑ C Ⓓ Ⓖ

The trunkless Dwarf Grass Tree has many arching leaves to 1 m long and a flowering stem 1–1.5 m long with a short cream flower spike to 10 cm resembling a banksia flower. This handsome little grass tree makes an excellent specimen for a rockery, frequently producing several flower spikes in spring. It will accept a little shade. Frost hardy. Propagate from seed.

Grasses

With more than 1400 species of grasses in the Australian flora, it is surprising that we have been unable to find a suitable species to use as a lawn. However, several are of value as ornamentals because of their attractive flowerheads. Management of grasses always provides some challenges as most produce considerable quantities of viable seed. Care must be taken to remove the flowerheads before the seed matures to prevent the plant becoming a weed.

Kangaroo Grass · *Themeda australis*   *All Zones*

Kangaroo Grass is probably the most widespread native grass in the Australian flora, occupying habitats from coastal headlands to forests and even sub-alpine areas, and occurring in all States. It is a hardy tussocky grass with soft leaves to 30 cm long and an interesting nodding flower spike to 80 cm in spring and summer. Kangaroo Grass does not usually present a weed problem. It prefers full sun and may be used to add interest to a rockery. Most soils are suitable.

Swamp Foxtail · *Pennisetum alopecuroides*   *All Zones*

This tufted species has arching narrow leaves to 80 cm and feathery heads of greenish pink to purplish flowers present for much of the year. They are suitable for floral arrangements. Care must be taken with this species to remove the flowerheads before the seed matures. Most soils are suitable. Prefers full sun. It will not tolerate very heavy frosts. Propagate from seed. (A very weedy South African species is sometimes sold under this name.)

• Common Grass Tree *Xanthorrhoea australis*

• Dwarf Grass Tree *Xanthorrhoea macronema*

• Kangaroo Grass *Themeda australis*

• Swamp Foxtail *Pennisetum alopecuroides*

Grevilleas

 With more than 340 species, Grevillea *is the third largest genus in the Australian flora. It is also one of the most popular with gardeners. Grevilleas can be found in most habitats and because of this a species can be found for your garden no matter where you live. Many hybrids are also commercially available. Most grevilleas flower best in a sunny situation with reasonably good drainage. There are species or cultivars for any situation, ranging in form from ground covers to small or large shrubs and tall trees. Many species are frost hardy. Propagation is easy from cuttings.*

Elegance · *Grevillea* 'Elegance'   *Zones:* B D E G
Sometimes called 'Long John', this hybrid forms an erect shrub 3 m by 3 m, with glossy, finely divided leaves and reddish stems. The waxy red flowers are borne at the ends of the branches and in the leaf axils from late winter to early summer. This is one of the best grevilleas. Plants grafted on to hardy rootstock are available, increasing its reliability in the garden. It is very attractive to nectar-seeking birds. Frost tender.

Honey Gem · *Grevillea* 'Honey Gem'   *Zones:* B D E F
One of the most popular cultivars for warmer areas, this plant virtually never stops flowering. It can reach up to 8 m in height but through regular pruning may be kept to 4 m high by 4 m across. Pruning also helps to improve the shape of the plant and increase its flowering. The leaves are silvery on the underside and the orange flowers are borne in semi-cylindrical sprays to 16 cm long throughout the year. Honeyeaters and lorikeets enjoy the ample nectar. Frost tender.

Moonlight · *Grevillea* 'Moonlight'   *Zones:* B D E F
This tall cultivar may reach 5 m by 4 m but can be restrained in size by pruning. It has silvery grey divided leaves and cylindrical spikes of cream or almost white flowers, about 16 cm long. Flowers appear over most of the year. Frost tender.

Poorinda Royal Mantle · *Grevillea* 'Poorinda Royal Mantle'   *All Zones*
Probably the best ground-cover grevillea, this hardy, totally prostrate plant has been seen to grow well in most parts of Australia. To cover a bank or similar area, it should be planted 2–3 m apart. The red toothbrush-like flowers appear mainly in late winter and spring but occasional blooms may be produced at other times. Honeyeaters seek out the flowers. Prefers full sun. Frost hardy.

• **Elegance** *Grevillea* 'Elegance'

• **Honey Gem** *Grevillea* 'Honey Gem'

• **Moonlight** *Grevillea* 'Moonlight'

• **Poorinda Royal Mantle** *Grevillea* 'Poorinda Royal Mantle'

Robyn Gordon • *Grevillea* 'Robyn Gordon'   Zones: A B D G H

One of the most famous grevillea hybrids, this plant was bred in southern inland Queensland; the original plant is still alive more than 30 years later. Robyn Gordon forms a rounded shrub to 1 m high by 1.5 m across and its red flowers appear throughout the year, borne in pendent sprays about 12 cm long. Frost hardy.

Alpine Grevillea • *Grevillea alpina*   Zones: A B C

An excellent plant for temperate areas, the Alpine Grevillea is very variable in form and careful selection is important to ensure that you get the particular flower colour and shape of shrub that you want. The colour of the late winter to spring flowers varies from yellow to red, yellow and red, yellow and white, pink and white, red and white or pink. Some forms are almost prostrate while others may reach almost 2 m in height. Look at the plant label or ask nursery staff for advice. This species is not at home in humid areas, so in Zone B you should ensure there is plenty of air movement around the plant. Frost hardy.

Bailey's Grevillea or White Oak • *Grevillea baileyana*   Zones: B D E F

Bailey's Grevillea is a rainforest tree and is only suitable for large gardens or rural properties as it will reach 25 m in height. It is, however, an outstanding tree with leaves that are dark green on the top and shiny bronze on the reverse. The foliage was used in the presentation bouquets at the Sydney 2000 Olympic Games. The white flowers, which appear in early summer, are also spectacular. Frost tender.

Banks' Grevillea • *Grevillea banksii*   Zones: B D E F G

This is a very reliable, long-flowering species with dark green divided leaves and bright red cylindrical flower spikes appearing throughout the year. It forms a tall shrub to 3 m high by 2.5 m across. Regular pruning will improve its shape. White-flowering forms are also available. This is a very hardy shrub for frost-free areas.

Prostrate Grevillea • *Grevillea curviloba* ssp. *incurva*   Zones: A B C G

Although usually prostrate in form, this handsome grevillea will occasionally produce a more upright branch to 1 m or more that may be pruned off. The plant will spread to 2 m in diameter. It has light green divided leaves and produces masses of fragrant white spidery flowers in late winter and spring. Good drainage is important and full sun gives the best flowering. Frost hardy. It is often sold incorrectly in nurseries as *Grevillea biternata*.

Mt Brockman Grevillea • *Grevillea formosa*   Zones: D E F G H

Found naturally in Kakadu National Park, this wonderful grevillea has become popular for use in warmer gardens in recent years. It has silvery grey, finely divided leaves and produces yellow flower spikes, which may reach 30 cm in length, from late summer to winter. One plant will cover at least 2 square metres. Grafted plants, often considered more reliable, are available from nurseries. Full sun and good drainage are recommended. Frost tender.

• Robyn Gordon *Grevillea* 'Robyn Gordon'

• Alpine Grevillea *Grevillea alpina*

• Bailey's Grevillea or White Oak *Grevillea baileyana*

• Banks' Grevillea *Grevillea banksii*

• Prostrate Grevillea *Grevillea curviloba* ssp. *incurva*

• Mt Brockman Grevillea *Grevillea formosa*

Woolly Grevillea • *Grevillea lanigera*   *Zones:* A B C

This shrub is variable in size but mostly reaches about 1 m high by about 80 cm across. It has grey-green hairy leaves and red and cream spidery flowers, borne in clusters at the ends of branches in late winter and spring. It is hardy in temperate climates but good drainage is important. It will grow in full to part sun. Frost hardy.

Lavender Grevillea • *Grevillea lavandulacea*   *Zones:* A B C

This compact little late winter- to spring-flowering shrub is variable in form and flower colour, although most forms will reach about 50 cm high by 50 cm across. Flowers range from pink to red with a little cream at the tip of the sepals. It may be used in rockeries or as a container plant for a patio or verandah. Good drainage and full to part sun are recommended. Frost hardy.

Plume Grevillea • *Grevillea leucopteris*   *Zones:* A G H

This shrub is rounded in form, to about 2 m by 2 m. The foliage is grey and much divided. The tall branching flowering stems rise to 4 m in height, producing plumes of creamy white, strongly perfumed flowers in spring. Not everyone enjoys the perfume and it has been given the unfortunate name of 'Old Socks'. The stems should be allowed to remain after flowering as the following year they will produce more flowers. Although best suited to areas with winter rainfall, grafted plants are sometimes available and these will survive on the east coast. Good drainage and full sun are recommended. Frost tender.

Silky Oak • *Grevillea robusta*   *Zones:* A B C D E F G

The Silky Oak is a tall tree to 30 m in height, with fern-like foliage and golden flowers in spring. Although too big for the small suburban garden, it is a handsome tree for rural properties and parks. Birds are attracted to the nectar and it is hardy in most situations where adequate water is available. Silky Oak is used as a root stock for many Western Australian species. Grafting them onto this hardy and vigorous east coast species increases their adaptability in the eastern humid summers. In areas with very heavy frosts it may be partly deciduous. Propagate from seed.

Red Spider Flower • *Grevillea speciosa*   *Zones:* A B C D

Common in the Hawkesbury sandstone areas around Sydney, this medium-sized shrub will reach 1.5 m high by 1 m across. Its large red spidery flowers are well displayed and appear in late winter and spring. Regular pruning will help to control its often unruly shape. Reasonable drainage and full to half sun are recommended. Frost hardy.

• **Woolly Grevillea** *Grevillea lanigera*

• **Plume Grevillea** *Grevillea leucopteris*

• **Silky Oak** *Grevillea robusta*

• **Lavender Grevillea** *Grevillea lavandulacea*

• **Red Spider Flower** *Grevillea speciosa*

Guinea Flowers

Guinea flowers belong to the genus Hibbertia, which contains more than 110 species, most of them occurring naturally only in Australia. Most have open, five-petalled, bright yellow flowers which are at their best in spring and early summer. As guinea flowers require good drainage and tend to be either small shrubs or prostrate in form, they are excellent subjects for a rockery. Two of the hardiest species are described below.

Hairy Guinea Flower • Hibbertia vestita
Zones: **A** **B** D

A prostrate or slightly erect plant with narrow dark green leaves, this species will spread to about 50 cm across. Bright yellow flowers up to 3 cm in diameter cover the plant in spring. Full sun and a well-drained soil are recommended. This species is frequently found on coastal headlands in the wild and is resistant to salt spray. Slightly frost tender. Propagate from cuttings, which are best taken in early summer.

Stalked Guinea Flower • Hibbertia pedunculata
Zones: **A** **B** C D

Probably the hardiest of the shrubby guinea flowers, this species will form a rounded dwarf shrub about 40 cm high by 50 cm in diameter. The foliage is a shiny dark green that contrasts well with the bright yellow flowers, up to 1.5 cm in diameter, which are borne prolifically from spring through summer. Most soils are suitable, in a full sun or part shade situation. Frost hardy. Propagate from cuttings.

Gymea Lily

'Gymea' is an Aboriginal name for this fascinating plant. It naturally occurs from the Sydney area to the north coast of New South Wales. The Aborigines used to roast the young stems and roots before eating them. In recent years this species has gained popularity and is now often seen in roadside and median strip plantings. Heavy frost will damage flowers.

Gymea Lily • Doryanthes excelsa
Zones: **A** **B** C D G

This unique plant forms a tall clump of sword-like leaves to 2 m long, extending to 3 m across as the plant ages. The immense flower spike rises to 6 m and bears at its apex a large cluster of bright red flowers. Each flower is up to 10 cm in diameter and they open continuously over many months. The flower spikes are often used in large floral arrangements. Gymea Lily may take about six years to flower from seed but after this it flowers each year, sometimes developing multiple flower spikes. Most situations are suitable.

• **Hairy Guinea Flower** *Hibbertia vestita*

• **Stalked Guinea Flower** *Hibbertia pedunculata*

• **Gymea Lily** *Doryanthes excelsa*

Hakeas

The genus Hakea *is a member of the protea family and is endemic to Australia. More than 140 species are recognised. These small to medium-sized woody shrubs or occasionally small trees sometimes have very prickly foliage. Most are very showy in flower. They feature interestingly shaped woody fruits which remain on the shrub. Most are hardy in cultivation and thrive in a full sun position in reasonably well-drained soil. Propagation is easiest from seed, which is readily collected once the woody fruits have matured for at least 12 months. The fruits should be left in a dry warm spot for a few days until the two seeds pop out. Germination may take two to five weeks.*

Baker's Hakea • *Hakea bakeriana*   *Zones:* A B C D G

Forming a shrub to 2 m high by 2 m across, this species is long lived in cultivation. The bright green needle-like leaves are about 7 cm long and the pink and white flowers are borne prolifically on the old wood in winter. Although the flowers are slightly hidden, they are popular with nectar-seeking birds, and judicious pruning will make them more visible. The woody fruits are very large, up to 5 cm in diameter. Most soils and full to half sun are recommended. Frost hardy.

Red Pokers • *Hakea bucculenta*   *Zones:* A C G H

This is an erect shrub to 4 m high by 2 m across with long narrow leaves to 17 cm. The red flowers are borne in tapering spikes to 15 cm long and appear in winter. They are borne on the old wood. The grey woody fruits, about 2 cm long, are borne in clusters. This species requires excellent drainage and full sun and is not suited to the humid east coast. Frost hardy.

Grass-leaf Hakea • *Hakea multilineata*   *Zones:* A C G H

A medium-sized shrub to 4 m high by 3 m across with oblong leaves to 20 cm long, this plant produces clusters of flowers in the leaf axils. They vary in colour from pale to deep pink and appear in winter and spring. The grey woody fruits, about 2 cm long, are borne in clusters of 8–10. In windy situations it may be best to stake this shrub as it is prone to blowing over. Frost hardy.

Silky Hakea • *Hakea sericea*   *Zones:* A B C D

This popular hakea is sometimes known as Needle Bush for its sharply pointed leaves, which make it an excellent screen plant. It will reach 2–3 m high by 2 m across. Flowers are borne in small sprays in the leaf axils in spring and are normally white, although pink forms are available. The fruits are large and prominent. This shrub is very hardy in most soils and aspects. Frost hardy.

• Baker's Hakea *Hakea bakeriana*

• Red Pokers *Hakea bucculenta*

• Grass-leaf Hakea *Hakea multilineata*

• Silky Hakea *Hakea sericea*

Heaths

Heath is a name given to a plant community of small woody shrubs and herbs, often occurring on poor sandy coastal soils. It is also applied to members of the family Epacridaceae, which frequently occur in these communities. This family is very diverse and includes many beautiful flowering plants, a lot of which, unfortunately, are not easy to grow in the garden. Two of the easier species, which are well worth trying, are described below.

Native Fuchsia • *Epacris longiflora* *Zones:* A B C D

This handsome little shrub is best grown in a rockery where drainage is good. It forms a sprawling shrub to 80 cm high by 60 cm across with long red and white tubular bells produced throughout the year. Each flower is about 2.5 cm long. The small triangular leaves are sharply pointed. It will accept some shade or full sun; a good layer of mulch is advisable to prevent its fine roots from drying out. Frost hardy. Propagate from cuttings.

Common Heath • *Epacris impressa* *Zones:* A B C

Victoria's floral emblem is a variable shrub in both form and flower colour. It may reach about 1 m high as a straggly shrub but with regular pruning can be controlled to a more rounded form. Flower colour varies from white through pinks to bright red. The flowers are tubular to about 1.5 cm long and may be seen in most months, although a flush in spring can be expected. Good drainage and a little shade are preferred. Frost hardy. Propagate from cuttings.

Hibiscus and Their Relatives

Free-flowering warm-climate members of the worldwide mallow family, Australia's native hibiscus are fast-growing plants. They may become leggy if not kept in shape by regular pruning.

Lilac Hibiscus • *Alyogyne huegelii* *Zones:* A B C G H

This hardy species forms a shrub to 2 m high by 1.5 m across with deeply lobed leaves to 6 cm long. The lilac-coloured hibiscus-like flowers are about 12 cm in diameter and appear in spring and summer. Regular pruning will keep the plant compact and encourage flowering. A sunny position is required but most soils are suitable. Reasonably frost hardy. Propagate from seed or cuttings.

• Native Fuchsia *Epacris longiflora*

• Common Heath *Epacris impressa*

• Lilac Hibiscus *Alyogyne huegelii*

Native Rosella • *Hibiscus heterophyllus*

Zones: A B D E F G

A tall open shrub or small tree, this fast-growing plant may reach 6 m in height but can be kept smaller by regular pruning. The leaves vary in shape and the flowers may be white with a dark centre, pink or sometimes yellow. Each flower is about 10–12 cm in diameter. The main flowering season is spring and summer. Most soils and aspects are suitable. Slightly frost tender. Propagate from seed or cuttings.

Hollyhock Tree • *Hibiscus splendens*

Zones: A B D E F G

A fast-growing shrub which can reach up to 4 m high by 3 m across, the Hollyhock Tree has grey-green leaves which are sparsely prickly, and lolly pink flowers about 12 cm across borne in spring and summer. Most soils and aspects are suitable, but the plant may be damaged in areas subject to heavy frosts. Tiny flea beetles may damage the foliage and flowers but can be controlled with common insecticides. Propagate from seed.

Cottonwood • *Hibiscus tiliaceus*

Zones: D E F

This small spreading tree reaches 7 m in height with a shady crown spreading to 12 m. The heart-shaped leaves are about 12 cm across and the bright yellow flowers have a red centre. Flowering occurs in summer and autumn. Prefers a sandy soil in full sun and is resistant to salt-laden winds. Frost tender. Propagate from seed or cuttings.

Hop Bushes

Hop bushes belong to the genus Dodonaea. *The common name derives from the early settlers' use of some species as a substitute for real hops. There are over 60 species in Australia and while the flowers are insignificant, their interesting foliage and fruits make most species useful garden plants. Most are hardy and very drought resistant. Propagation is from cuttings.*

Fern-leaf Hop Bush • *Dodonaea boroniifolia*

Zones: A C G H

This hardy plant forms an open shrub to 2 m high by 1 m across. The small 4 cm leaves are divided into 6–10 shiny dark green leaflets and the four-cornered fruits ripen to various shades of red in summer and autumn. This plant responds to a sunny site with good drainage and is resistant to dry periods. Frost hardy. Propagate from cuttings.

Common Hop Bush • *Dodonaea viscosa*

Zones: A B C G H

A very variable shrub in form, leaf shape and fruit colour, the Common Hop Bush varies in height from 1 m to 5 m; leaves may be anything from 1 cm to 15 cm long. Fruits mature in early summer and may be brown, pink, red or purple in colour. Check the plant label to be sure of which form you are buying. All forms are hardy in a sunny well-drained soil. The taller forms make useful screen plants. Frost hardy. Propagate from cuttings.

• Native Rosella *Hibiscus heterophyllus*

• Hollyhock Tree *Hibiscus splendens*

• Cottonwood *Hibiscus tiliaceus*

• Common Hop Bush *Dodonaea viscosa*

• Fern-leaf Hop Bush *Dodonaea boroniifolia*

Kangaroo Paws and Their Relatives

 Kangaroo paws occur naturally in the dry summer climate of Western Australia. In recent years plant breeders have produced a number of fine hybrids hardier than the original species, which are difficult to maintain in humid summer conditions. Several of these cultivars are described below. Nectar-seeking birds are attracted to the flowers. Most varieties make good cut flowers. A fungus known as ink disease may cause blackening of the leaves in some varieties. If this occurs, the plant is best destroyed.

Bush Gold · *Anigozanthos* 'Bush Gold'   Zones: A B D G

This fine clumping plant has sword-shaped leaves to 40 cm and branching spikes of golden flowers reaching about 80 cm high in spring and summer. The flowering stems are reddish. Good drainage and full sun offer the best conditions. This is a good cut flower and accent plant. Frost tender. Propagate by division.

Bush Ranger · *Anigozanthos* 'Bush Ranger'   Zones: A B G H

A dwarf cultivar with short leaves to 20 cm and miniature branching flower spikes to 40 cm. The spring flowers are bright red and clothed in red hairs. This plant is particularly fussy about drainage and a built-up rockery will be the best position. Full sun is also recommended. Frost tender. Propagate by division.

Dwarf Delight · *Anigozanthos* 'Dwarf Delight'   Zones: A B C D G

This hardy cultivar has leaves to 40 cm and rusty red branching flower spikes to 70 cm in spring. It is an outstanding plant and is probably the hardiest of all kangaroo paws in humid conditions. However, good drainage is still recommended, in full sun to part shade. Reasonably frost hardy. Propagate by division.

Red Cross · *Anigozanthos* 'Red Cross'   Zones: A B D G

This cultivar produces a tall clumping accent plant with dark green leaves to 50 cm and burgundy-coloured flowers in spring and early summer on tall branching stems to 160 cm high. The flowers are clothed in soft red hairs on the outside and inside are smooth and green. It is reliable in reasonably well-drained soils in full sun or part shade. Reasonably frost hardy. Propagate by division.

• **Bush Gold** *Anigozanthos* 'Bush Gold'

• **Bush Ranger** *Anigozanthos* 'Bush Ranger'

• **Dwarf Delight** *Anigozanthos* 'Dwarf Delight'

• **Red Cross** *Anigozanthos* 'Red Cross'

Common Kangaroo Paw • *Anigozanthos flavidus*   *Zones:* A B C D G

Many different colour forms have been selected from this very vigorous species. If you want a particular colour, it is a good idea to purchase a specimen in flower. Leaves are up to 1 m long and the branching spring and summer flower spikes up to 2 m tall. Flower colour varies from dull green to shades of red and orange. It will grow in most soils and aspects and is frost hardy. Propagate from seed or by division.

Black Kangaroo Paw • *Macropidia fuliginosa*   *Zones:* A C G H

This unique spring-flowering plant is one of the few truly black flowers in the Australian flora, and makes a good cut flower. The colour is generated by the thick masses of black hairs covering the green flowers. The inside of the flower is smooth and bright green. Although this plant is recommended for Zone C, site it out of reach of heavy frosts, as they will damage the flowers. Requires excellent drainage and prefers full sun. Propagate from seed or division.

Prickly Cottonheads • *Conostylis aculeata*   *Zones:* A B C G

A tufted plant with narrow strap-like leaves to 40 cm long, this hardy species will grow in most soils and aspects. The leaves are edged with stiff bristles, so select a planting position out of reach of bare legs. Clusters of long-lasting yellow hairy flowers are held at the ends of stems that may reach 45 cm in length. They appear in spring and early summer. Frost hardy. Propagate from seed.

Mat Cottonheads • *Conostylis stylidioides*   *Zones:* A B C G

This dwarf spreading plant, less than 15 cm high, produces runners to cover an area about 40 cm across. The leaves are up to 5 cm long and the masses of yellow flowers are borne in spring on the ends of 8 cm stems. It is an ideal rockery plant, requiring reasonable drainage and full to part sun. Frost hardy. Propagate by division of runners.

Kurrajongs

While noted for their drought-resistant qualities, members of this genus may be frost tender when young. One species, Brachychiton populneus, *has been widely planted in inland Australia for emergency stock fodder.*

Illawarra Flame Tree • *Brachychiton acerifolius*   *Zones:* A B D E

This tall, partly deciduous tree to 20 m in height makes a brilliant display in late spring and early summer when its red bell-shaped flowers are at their peak. It is best grown in full sun where its massed flowers can be clearly seen. The lobed leaves are shiny light green and up to 20 cm wide; in full leaf this tree has a shapely cone-shaped crown. It accepts most soils but is frost tender. Propagate from seed.

• **Common Kangaroo Paw** *Anigozanthos flavidus*

• **Black Kangaroo Paw** *Macropidia fuliginosa*

• **Prickly Cottonheads** *Conostylis aculeata*

• **Mat Cottonheads** *Conostylis stylidioides*

• **Illawarra Flame Tree** *Brachychiton acerifolius*

Little Kurrajong • *Brachychiton bidwillii* *Zones:* B D E F H

An open deciduous shrub to 3 m in height, this plant bears its deep rose pink flowers in clusters along the old wood in winter (dry season) when it is leafless. Each flower is tubular and clothed in short hairs. The softly hairy leaves are lobed and about 12 cm across. This drought-resistant species prefers a well-drained soil in a warm sunny site. Frost tender. Propagate from cuttings.

Kurrajong • *Brachychiton populneus* *Zones:* A B C D G H

A handsome drought-resistant evergreen tree, the Kurrajong develops a rounded crown and will reach 20 m in height at maturity. The more or less heart-shaped leaves are bright green and about 10 cm wide. Flowers are cream, bell-shaped and borne in summer. Full sun and most soils are accepted. Frost hardy. Propagate from seed.

Bottle Tree • *Brachychiton rupestris* *All Zones*

With its swollen bottle-shaped trunk this tree is something of an inland icon, but it will also grow well at the coast. The leaves of the young trees are compound with three to nine leaflets, but the mature leaves are simple and lance-shaped. The summer flowers are small and not spectacular but the plant is worth growing for its interesting form. Slow growing, the Bottle Tree requires good drainage and will accept dry conditions. Frost hardy. Propagate from seed.

Leatherwood

 Leatherwood belongs to the genus Eucryphia, *of which there are four species occurring along the east coast of Australia and two in Chile, providing evidence that the continents were once joined as Gondwana. Of the two Tasmanian species, Leatherwood is common in the south-west of the State in the high-rainfall temperate rainforests. The other Tasmanian species is a medium-sized shrub, and a mainland species occurs as a tree in temperate rainforest. These are not generally available commercially.*

Leatherwood • *Eucryphia lucida* *Zones:* A B C

Native to Tasmania, this beautiful small tree requires a cool location with a little shade. It will reach 7 m in favourable conditions. The oblong leaves are about 4 cm long and the fragrant white flowers with red-tipped stamens, resembling a single rose, appear in spring and summer. The blossoms are popular with apiarists for the production of leatherwood honey. A well-mulched loamy soil is best. Frost hardy. Propagate from cuttings.

• Little Kurrajong *Brachychiton bidwillii*

• Kurrajong *Brachychiton populneus*

• Bottle Tree *Brachychiton rupestris*

• Leatherwood *Eucryphia lucida*

Lilies and Their Relatives

*The term 'lily' applies loosely to those plants that have a single seed leaf,
usually have attractive flowers and in some cases go dormant in winter.
These days botanists have divided them into a number of different
families, but for the sake of simplicity we have grouped them together here, as
their cultivation requirements and uses are generally similar.*

Bulbine Lily • *Bulbine bulbosa*
Zones: A B C D G

A bulbous plant with succulent leaves to about 40 cm and a spike of yellow star-shaped
flowers up to 50 cm long. The flowers, about 2.5 cm in diameter, appear in spring and
summer. Most soils and aspects are satisfactory and the plant often regenerates from
seed. Its long flowering period makes it an excellent rockery plant. Frost hardy.
Propagate from seed.

Garland Lily • *Calostemma purpureum*
Zones: A B C D G H

This bulbous plant is deciduous, with the flower stem emerging in early summer, usually
before the strap-like leaves. The dark green leaves are up to 40 cm long and the flower
spike will also reach the same height. The wine-red flowers are grouped at the end of the
stems in clusters of 12 or more. Full sun or part shade is recommended and most soils are
suitable. Ease off the watering when the plant goes dormant in winter. Frost hardy.
Propagate from seed or division as new bulbs are formed.

Swamp Lily • *Crinum pedunculatum*
Zones: B D E F G

This large evergreen species forms an erect plant with broad leaves reaching 1 m long. A
robust spike, 80 cm long, of large white flowers arises from the lower leaf axils. The 10 cm
fragrant flowers have slender petals and appear in spring and summer. This hardy species
will grow in most soils, even those that are saturated, and will accept full sun or shade.
Salt winds do not affect it but it may not tolerate heavy frosts. Propagate from seed.

Chocolate Lily • *Dichopogon strictus*
Zones: A B C D G H

It is worth growing this species for its perfume alone. The small mauve spring flowers,
borne on a slender stem to 40 cm long, have the most delightful chocolate perfume,
noticeable some metres away on a hot day. Grow several plants together for maximum
effect. The grass-like leaves die down over the warmer months. Most soils are suitable but
it prefers a sunny site. Frost hardy. Propagate from seed.

• Bulbine Lily *Bulbine bulbosa*

• Garland Lily *Calostemma purpureum*

• Swamp Lily *Crinum pedunculatum*

• Chocolate Lily *Dichopogon strictus*

Stream Lily · *Helmholtzia glaberrima*   *Zones:* B D E

This flax-like plant has bright green leaves to 1.5 m long. In summer it produces a plume of pinkish flowers on a stem to 1.5 m long. It is a spectacular plant for a moist shady site in a rich loamy soil. Frost tender. Propagate from seed or by division.

Native Jonquil · *Proiphys cunninghamii*   *Zones:* A B D E F G

This bulbous plant is dormant during the winter and produces its spade-shaped leaves to 40 cm long in spring. A spike of white flowers resembling jonquils appears in late spring. It is best grown in a shady spot, with well-composted soil. Tolerates mild frosts. Propagate from seed.

Vanilla Lily · *Sowerbaea juncea*   *Zones:* A B D

Named for its vanilla-like perfume, this little plant makes a delightful addition to the rockery. It appreciates ample water in the summer growing season. It is a tufted plant with rush-like leaves to 30 cm and spikes of mauve flowers in spring. Several flowering stems will be produced on well-established plants. Good drainage is important. Tolerates light frosts. Propagate by division.

Yellow Rush Lily · *Tricoryne elatior*   *Zones:* A B C D G H

This small tufted plant may reach 30 cm high and has grass-like leaves and slender stems of bright yellow flowers in summer. The flowers are about 2 cm in diameter. Most soils are suitable and full sun is preferred. It is a good rockery plant with several specimens planted together giving the best effect. Frost hardy. Propagate from seed.

Lilly Pillies

The name 'lilly pilly' is applied to a number of rainforest plants that belong to the genus Syzygium *and a few closely related genera. They are all hardy and attractive trees, some small, some large, with fluffy flowers and colourful, mostly edible fruits. They are best suited to tropical and subtropical areas where they may be used as screen plants or for hedges.*

Lilly Pilly · *Acmena smithii*   *Zones:* A B D E

A medium-sized tree with branches to the ground, this species is popular as a screen plant that is resistant to salt winds. It is an excellent tree for beachside suburbs. The small fluffy white summer flowers are followed by globular pink fruits maturing in autumn. They are edible and can be made into tasty jam. Most soils and aspects are suitable except where heavy frosts are common. Propagate from fresh seed.

• Stream Lily *Helmholtzia glaberrima*

• Native Jonquil *Proiphys cunninghamii*

• Vanilla Lily *Sowerbaea juncea*

• Yellow Rush Lily *Tricoryne elatior*

• Lilly Pilly *Acmena smithii*

Woolgoolga or Brush Cherry • *Syzygium australe*   *Zones:* B D E

Common in coastal rainforests, this shiny-leaved medium-sized tree to 10 m high may also be used as a screen from salty winds. The flowers are white and borne in prominent sprays in spring and the edible fruits are more or less pear-shaped, pink or red, and about 2.5 cm long. Although most soils and aspects are suitable, it is frost tender. Propagate from fresh seed.

Riberry • *Syzygium luehmannii*   *Zones:* B D E

This is a tall tree to 25 m high with handsome foliage, flowers and fruits. It is a little large for the average suburban garden but an excellent plant for rural properties or parks. The foliage is light green and shiny and the young growth is vivid pink. The spring or summer flowers are fluffy and white and the edible fruits are red and pear-shaped. Most soils and aspects in frost-free areas are suitable. Propagate from seed.

Powderpuff Lilly Pilly • *Syzygium wilsonii* ssp. *wilsonii*   *Zones:* B D E F

This is a medium-sized shrub to 2 m high by 1.5 m across. The young growth is bright pink and pendulous and the large powderpuff flowers, maroon and about 10 cm in diameter, hang from the branch tips in spring and early summer. The fruits are pure white and offer a contrast to the foliage. Prefers some shade and a well-mulched loamy soil. Frost tender. Propagate from seed or cuttings.

Lobelias

 There are about 20 native lobelias; some are annual and others perennial. The two perennial types given here are well worth a spot in any garden. Lobelias generally appreciate ample water and most prefer some shade.

Mat Lobelia • *Lobelia membranacea*   *Zones:* A B D E

This dainty prostrate species spreads to about 50 cm. It has tiny 5 mm leaves and masses of light blue flowers in spring and summer. It grows best in damp soil with a little shade. In ideal conditions it will layer itself. It will tolerate at least light frosts. Propagate from seed or removal of layered pieces.

Trailing Lobelia • *Lobelia trigonocaulis*   *Zones:* B D E

The stems of this slender trailing plant with toothed heart-shaped leaves will reach 50 cm. The flowers vary in colour from light to dark blue or even white and are borne prolifically on long stalks to 10 cm in spring and summer. This species prefers a low light situation with ample moisture. It makes a good basket plant as well as a plant for a shady rockery. Frost tender. Propagate from seed or cuttings.

• Woolgoolga or Brush Cherry *Syzygium australe*

• Riberry *Syzygium luehmannii*

• Mat Lobelia *Lobelia membranacea*

• Powderpuff Lilly Pilly *Syzygium wilsonii*
ssp. *wilsonii*

• Trailing Lobelia *Lobelia trigonocaulis*

Lomatias

Lomatias belong to the prolific protea family and occur naturally in eastern Australia and South America. There are nine Australian species. All have attractive shiny or much-divided foliage and fragrant cream flowers producing ample nectar.

Tree Lomatia • *Lomatia arborescens*
Zones: A B C D E

This plant may reach 6 m but can be easily kept to shrub proportions of about 3 m high by 2 m across by regular pruning. The glossy green leaves are toothed and about 14 cm long. The cream flowers are borne in sprays to 15 cm in summer. It grows best in part or heavy shade in a well-composted loamy soil. Frost hardy. Propagate from seed or cuttings.

Black-leaved Silky Oak • *Lomatia fraxinifolia*
Zones: B D E F

A handsome small to medium-sized tree with large, much-divided, dark green, glossy leaves, up to 50 cm long on juvenile specimens but shortening as the plant ages. They blacken when they fall to the ground. The light cream flowers are borne in branching sprays in summer. Most well-drained loamy soils are suitable. It will grow in full sun or part shade. Probably frost tender. Propagate from seed.

Wild Parsley • *Lomatia silaifolia*
Zones: A B C D G

This plant forms an erect shrub to 1.5 m high with very variable leaves. Some forms have finely divided leaves vaguely reminiscent of parsley, others have much coarser leaves. The creamy white flowers are borne in summer on long branching sprays held above the foliage. The seed pods are attractive and may be used in floral arrangements. A well-drained soil in part shade is preferred. Frost hardy. Propagate from seed.

Mat Rushes

Strap-leaved quick-growing perennials, mat rushes are very low maintenance plants in the right conditions. Male and female flowers are borne on separate plants. The species are frequently confused.

Slender Mat Rush • *Lomandra hystrix*
Zones: A B D E F G

This large tufted plant has dark green arching leaves to 1.5 m long. The small greenish flowers are borne on stiff stems to 1 m long in spring. This species grows well in damp soil and is ideal for placing near a water feature where its leaves will arch into the water. Appreciates some shade. Frost hardy. Propagate from seed.

• **Tree Lomatia** *Lomatia arborescens*

• **Black-leaved Silky Oak** *Lomatia fraxinifolia*

• **Wild Parsley** *Lomatia silaifolia*

• **Slender Mat Rush** *Lomandra hystrix*

Long-leaved Mat Rush · *Lomandra longifolia*   *Zones:* A B C D H

Despite its common name, the leaves of this species are shorter than those of the Slender Mat Rush, reaching up to 70 cm but often less. It is more resistant to dry conditions and is often used on road median strips. The crowded flower spikes are borne on flattened stems in summer. Most soils and aspects are suitable. Frost hardy. Propagate from seed.

Melaleucas and Their Relatives

 Several genera in the Australian flora are closely related to Melaleuca, *being separated by minor botanical differences in their flower structure. For the sake of simplicity we have dealt with them together, as many may be treated similarly in cultivation. For more information, refer to our book* Bottlebrushes, Paperbarks & Tea Trees *(Angus & Robertson 1993), which describes all species in detail.*

Brass's Honey-myrtle · *Asteromyrtus brassii*   *Zones:* D E F

Occurring naturally on Cape York, this species also grows and flowers well in the subtropics. It will reach 10 m in good garden conditions but will be reduced to a tall shrub on exposed sites. With neat mid-green foliage and fluffy red globular flowers about golf-ball size, it is hardy in most soils and aspects. Birds are attracted to the flowers, which are produced from May to October on the old wood. Frost tender. Propagate from seed or cuttings.

Swamp Bottlebrush · *Beaufortia sparsa*   *Zones:* A C G

This medium-sized, sparsely branched shrub will reach at least 2 m in height, with small neat foliage and deep orange flowers resembling a bottlebrush carried close to the ends of the long branches in summer and autumn. Despite its common name, it grows best in well-drained soil, in full to part sun. Frost hardy. Propagate from seed or cuttings.

Round-leaf Eremaea · *Eremaea beaufortioides*   *Zones:* A C G

This rounded shrub with neat small leaves will reach 2.5 m high by 2.5 m across and produces fluffy orange flowers, about 2.5 cm diameter, at the ends of its branchlets in spring. It requires excellent drainage and prefers full sun. Frost hardy. Propagate from seed.

Tick Bush · *Kunzea ambigua*   *Zones:* A B C D G H

The unflattering common name is not really deserved, as it is unlikely that this shrub attracts ticks any more than others do. It is, however, a very hardy shrub, which will accept most soils and aspects. It is even resistant to salt-laden winds. This makes it a fine screen or shelter plant, reaching at least 3 m high by 3 m across, and making a good display of fluffy white or mauve flowers in late spring and early summer. Frost hardy. Propagate from cuttings.

• Long-leaved Mat Rush *Lomandra longifolia*

• Brass's Honey Myrtle *Asteromyrtus brassii*

• Swamp Bottlebrush *Beaufortia sparsa*

• Round-leaf Eremaea *Eremaea beaufortioides*

• Tick Bush *Kunzea ambigua*

Scarlet Kunzea • *Kunzea baxteri*
Zones: A B C G H

Spectacular in flower, this large shrub will reach 3 m high by 3 m across and requires a well-drained sunny site. The leaves are bright green, about 1.5 cm long, and the brilliant red bottlebrush-like flowers are tipped with yellow anthers. They are borne in spring. It may be slow to produce its first flowers. Frost hardy. Propagate from cuttings

Heath Kunzea • *Kunzea capitata*
Zones: A B C D

Common in the east coast heathlands, this small shrub is usually less than 1 m high. The small leaves are slightly hairy and the mauve-pink fluffy flowers are borne near the ends of branches in spring and summer. Reasonable drainage and full to part sun give the best results. Frost hardy. Propagate from cuttings.

Muntries • *Kunzea pomifera*
Zones: A C G H

This prostrate plant spreading to about 1 m is ideal for dry sandy soils. It has small, rounded, bright green leaves less than 1 cm long. The fluffy white flowers which appear in spring contrast well with the foliage. Full sun is preferred. The cream globular fruits are succulent and attractive to birds. Frost hardy. Propagate from cuttings.

Granite Kunzea • *Kunzea pulchella*
Zones: A C G H

Occurring on the huge granite outcrops of Western Australia, this beautiful shrub reaches 3 m high by 3 m across. The grey-green leaves are clothed with silky hairs and contrast well with the brilliant red flowers, which are borne at the ends of short side branches in spring. Excellent drainage and relatively dry summers are required but the shrub is frost hardy. Propagate from seed or cuttings.

Barrens Regelia • *Regelia velutina*
Zones: A C G

Occurring in the Barrens Range in Western Australia, this shrub is one of the most beautiful in the Australian flora. Its erect conifer-like habit and its neat silvery green foliage are both attractive features, but its bright scarlet-red fluffy spring flowers borne at the ends of the branches make it quite outstanding. It may not flower for the first few years of its life. Excellent drainage and full sun are recommended. Frost hardy. Propagate from seed.

• Scarlet Kunzea *Kunzea baxteri*

• Heath Kunzea *Kunzea capitata*

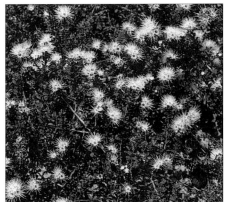

• Muntries *Kunzea pomifera*

• Granite Kunzea *Kunzea pulchella*

• Barrens Regelia *Regelia velutina*

MELALEUCAS

The genus Melaleuca *is by far the largest in this group, with about 250 species. Some are trees with papery bark that peels off in sheets, commonly known as paperbarks. Others are shrubs with nectar-laden flowers, often known as honey-myrtles. Small individual flowers are grouped together form fluffy clusters or bottlebrush-like spikes. Almost all melaleucas have great horticultural merit and are relatively easy to grow.*

Snow-in-summer · *Melaleuca alternifolia*   *Zones:* A B C D E G
This species forms a medium-sized shrub or small tree to 8 m. Its bright green aromatic foliage is used for the extraction of tea-tree oil, which has a number of therapeutic uses. It bears a profusion of fluffy white flowers in late spring and summer. It is ideal for a damp spot and will tolerate full sun or part shade. Frost hardy. Propagate from seed or cuttings.

Silver-leaved Paperbark · *Melaleuca argentea*   *Zones:* D E F H
Occurring naturally in or near swamps in tropical areas, this tall handsome tree has pendulous branches bearing long grey-green leaves and papery bark. Although recommended for Zone H, it requires ample water to thrive. The greenish-cream flowers are borne in long bottlebrush-like spikes in winter and spring. Frost tender. Propagate from seed.

Bracelet Honey-myrtle · *Melaleuca armillaris*   *Zones:* A B C D
Commonly grown as a windbreak, this large spreading shrub tolerates exposure to salt-laden winds. It usually reaches 5–6 m in height with branches to the ground. The small bottlebrush flowers are usually white but pink forms are available. Flowers occur in groups up to 7 cm long mostly in spring and early summer. Hardy to mild frosts. Propagation is easy from seed or cuttings. Saw-fly larvae, caterpillars that tend to gather together in large groups, may cause severe defoliation. Remove them by hand and squash, or spray them with Malathion®.

Cross-leaved Honey-myrtle · *Melaleuca decussata*   *Zones:* A B C D H
One of the hardiest melaleucas for temperate areas, this open shrub reaches 2 m high by 1.5 m across. The neat leaves are arranged in two pairs of opposite rows, giving the shrub its common name. The flowers are pale mauve, borne in small bottlebrush spikes about 2 cm long in late spring and summer. Most soils and aspects are suitable. Frost hardy. Propagate from seed.

Granite Honey-myrtle · *Melaleuca elliptica*   *Zones:* A B C D E G H
A medium-sized shrub, usually less than 3 m high by 2 m across, this Western Australian species is adaptable to the east coast. It has small rounded leaves, to 12 mm long, and large red bottlebrush flowers in late spring and summer. Most reasonably drained soils are suitable. Prefers full sun. Frost hardy. Propagate from seed.

• Snow-in-summer *Melaleuca alternifolia*

• Silver-leaved Paperbark *Melaleuca argentea*

• Cross-leaved Honey-myrtle *Melaleuca decussata*

• Bracelet Honey-myrtle *Melaleuca armillaris*

• Granite Honey-myrtle *Melaleuca elliptica*

Wiry Honey-myrtle • *Melaleuca filifolia*   *Zones:* A B G H

This medium-sized shrub to 3 m high by 2.5 m across has thin leaves to 10 cm long. It bears mauve-pink flowers in clusters at the ends of branches in spring. Each flower group is about 4 cm in diameter. Good drainage and a sunny site are recommended. Frost tender. Propagate from seed.

Scarlet Honey-myrtle • *Melaleuca fulgens*   *Zones:* A B G H

Varying in height from 50 cm to 2 m, this handsome shrub produces large fluffy flowers about 3 cm across in spring. The colour is usually red, but apricot and pink forms are also available, the apricot form being particularly attractive. Birds are attracted to the flowers. Good drainage and full sun are important and it will tolerate light frosts. Propagate from seed or cuttings.

Hillock Bush • *Melaleuca hypericifolia*   *Zones:* A B C D G H

This medium-sized shrub rarely exceeds 2 m high by 2 m across and bears its flowers on the old wood. Foliage is neat but pruning of in-growing branches makes it easier to see the flowers. They are rusty red bottlebrushes about 6 cm long and 5 cm diameter, appreciated by birds and appearing in late spring and summer. Hardy in most soils and situations, but will be damaged by heavy frosts. Propagate from seed.

Grey Honey-myrtle • *Melaleuca incana*   *Zones:* A B C G H

This erect shrub will reach 3 m high by 2 m across, with pendulous branches and grey-green, softly hairy leaves. Creamy white bottlebrush flowers appear in spring. Good drainage and full to part sun are recommended. This species is subject to scale and the associated black smut, which may be controlled by spraying with white oil. Frost hardy. Propagate from seed.

Robin Redbreast Bush • *Melaleuca lateritia*   *Zones:* A B C G H

A small to medium-sized, open shrub rarely exceeding 1.5 m high by 1 m across, this hardy West Australian has adapted to the east coast in well-drained situations. Full sun is also recommended. The orange-red bottlebrush flowers are produced over much of the year, but are at their best in summer. They are borne on the old wood but the shrub is sufficiently open to make them well displayed. Frost hardy. Propagate from seed.

Weeping Paperbark • *Melaleuca leucadendra*   *Zones:* B D E F H

This medium-sized to large tree features papery bark, pendulous branches and long drooping leaves of variable width. The creamy white bottlebrush flowers are up to 8 cm long and seen mainly from autumn to spring. Although occurring naturally in swamps or along rivers in northern Australia, this species will adapt to drier locations as well. The narrow-leaved form is particularly ornamental, resembling a small weeping willow but without its invasive root system. Full sun or part shade. Frost tender. Propagate from seed.

• Wiry Honey-myrtle *Melaleuca filifolia*

• Scarlet Honey-myrtle *Melaleuca fulgens*

• Hillock Bush *Melaleuca hypericifolia*

• Grey Honey-myrtle *Melaleuca incana*

• Robin Redbreast Bush *Melaleuca lateritia*

• Weeping Paperbark *Melaleuca leucadendra*

Claw Flower · *Melaleuca pulchella* *Zones:* A B C G

This small shrub is one of the few melaleucas that bears its flowers singly. The individual spring flowers are large, and it is the inward-curving groups of anthers that give the plant its common name. Rarely exceeding 60 cm in height, this shrub does well in reasonably well-drained soils and most aspects. It makes an excellent rockery plant. Frost hardy. Propagate from seed or cuttings.

Broad-leaved Paperbark · *Melaleuca quinquenervia* *Zones:* B D E F H

This common tree occurs in swamps from around the Sydney area north to Cape York. It will reach about 20 m in height, with papery bark and cream summer bottlebrush flowers much favoured by nectar-seeking birds, particularly the colourful Rainbow Lorikeet. Red-flowered forms are available from nurseries and these are highly recommended. Most soils and aspects are suitable but the species is frost tender. Propagate from seed.

Graceful Honey-myrtle · *Melaleuca radula* *Zones:* A C G H

Growing 1–1.5 m high, this handsome small open shrub produces pink, mauve or purple fluffy flowers on the old wood. Flowering occurs in spring. Good drainage and full to part sun are recommended. Although grown occasionally on the east coast, it normally does not do well in humid summers. A hybrid between this species and Scarlet Honey-myrtle has deep-purple flowers. Frost hardy. Propagate from seed or cuttings.

Thyme-leaved Honey-myrtle · *Melaleuca thymifolia* *Zones:* A B C D G

This small shrub with a long spring and summer flowering period is highly recommended for most garden situations. Several cultivars selected for their extended flowering period and compact habit, mostly growing to about 50 cm, are available commercially. The mauve-pink or white flowers are borne in fluffy clusters on the old wood. Cultivars are known as 'Pink Lace' and 'White Lace'. This species is tolerant of most soils and aspects, and frost hardy. Propagate from seed or cuttings.

Violet Honey-myrtle · *Melaleuca wilsonii* *Zones:* A B C G H

A low spreading shrub to 1 m high by 2 m across, this shrub is spectacular in flower. The mauve-purple spring flowers are borne in extended spikes on the previous season's wood. The foliage is neat. Good drainage and a sunny position are recommended. Frost hardy. Propagate from seed.

• Claw Flower *Melaleuca pulchella*

• Broad-leaved Paperbark *Melaleuca quinquenervia*   • Graceful Honey-myrtle *Melaleuca radula*

• Thyme-leaved Honey-myrtle *Melaleuca thymifolia*   • Violet Honey-myrtle *Melaleuca wilsonii*

Mint Bushes and Their Relatives

 The mint bush family is characterised by tubular flowers with a prominent lower lip. Many have aromatic foliage, which adds a pleasant dimension to their use in the garden. The exotic household mint, which belongs to this family, is typical.

Austral Bugle • *Ajuga australis*   Zones: A B C D G H

This spreading plant forms rosettes of softly hairy leaves to 12 cm long. The leafy spikes of pink, mauve or purple flowers to 30 cm high arise from the centres of the rosettes in spring and summer. Plant 50 cm apart if you are using it as a ground cover. This hardy plant will grow in most soils in full sun or part shade. Frost hardy. Propagation is by division of suckers.

Alpine Mint Bush • *Prostanthera cuneata*   Zones: A B C

This low spreading plant will reach 1 m high by 1.5 m across. It has dark green rounded leaves and white flowers with purple spots in the throat appearing in summer. The flowers contrast well with the dark foliage. Excellent drainage and full sun are recommended. Frost hardy. Propagate from cuttings.

White Mint Bush • *Prostanthera nivea*   Zones: A B C H

An open shrub that benefits from tip pruning after flowering, this species will reach 2–3 m in height. The narrow leaves are light green and the flowers are usually white, although pale blue forms are also known. The flowers appear in spring. Excellent drainage and full sun are preferred. This plant may be grafted onto stock of Coastal Rosemary, *Westringia fruticosa*, to improve its longevity. Frost hardy. Propagate from cuttings.

Common Mint Bush • *Prostanthera ovalifolia*   Zones: A B C D H

This is the most commonly grown mint bush and one of the most beautiful in flower. It will reach 2 m in height and tip pruning after flowering will improve its shape. The flowers are purple and borne prolifically in spring. The foliage is aromatic. Excellent drainage and full sun or part shade are required. Grafting onto stock of Coastal Rosemary, *Westringia fruticosa*, will extend its life. Frost hardy. Propagate from cuttings.

Coastal Rosemary • *Westringia fruticosa*   Zones: A B C D G H

This rounded, spreading shrub is one of the hardiest in the Australian flora. It will reach 2 m in height and spread to 4 m, hugging the ground, to make an excellent screen. The grey-green leaves are about 2 cm long and the flowers are white and appear over most of the year. It will grow in most soils and aspects and is resistant to salt-laden coastal winds and frosts. Propagate from cuttings.

• **Austral Bugle** *Ajuga australis*

• **Common Mint Bush** *Prostanthera ovalifolia*

• **Alpine Mint Bush** *Prostanthera cuneata*

• **White Mint Bush** *Prostanthera nivea*

• **Coastal Rosemary** *Westringia fruticosa*

Wynyabbie Gem · *Westringia* 'Wynyabbie Gem'   *Zones:* A B C D G H

This cultivar is similar to *Westringia fruticosa* but more open in its habit and with pale lilac flowers, which are seen throughout the year. It is also very hardy in most soils and aspects and will benefit from regular pruning to maintain its shape. Frost hardy. Propagate from cuttings.

Mountain Bells and Their Relatives

 The genus Darwinia *includes about 40 species endemic to Australia, with flowers varying considerably in their appearance, although all are surrounded by a ring of bracts (petal-like structures). In some species the bracts are very large and colourful and give the flowers a bell-like appearance. These mountain bells occur naturally in the Stirling Ranges of Western Australia.*

Lemon-scented Myrtle · *Darwinia citriodora*   *Zones:* A B C G

This is a low spreading shrub to 1 m high by 1.5 m across, with grey-green, lemon-scented leaves on reddish stems. The bracts on the flowers are not prominent but the styles are long, starting out cream and aging to red. This is probably the hardiest of the Western Australian species, flowering in spring and summer. Good drainage and a little shade are preferred. Frost hardy. Propagate from cuttings.

Bundled Darwinia · *Darwinia fascicularis*   *Zones:* A B C D G H

The individual flowers of this species are 'bundled' together at the ends of branches, making the flowerhead about 1.5 cm in diameter. It is a small shrub, rarely exceeding 1 m high, with flowers that open white but age to red, giving a bicoloured effect. The bracts are small. Flowers appear in spring and early summer. Good drainage and full sun or part shade are recommended. Frost hardy. Propagate from cuttings.

Stirling's Bell · *Darwinia lejostyla*   *Zones:* A B G

Probably the most commonly cultivated of the mountain bells, this species occurs in the Stirling and Barren Ranges. This erect shrub will reach 1 m high, with neat small leaves and pendent bells of pink and white in spring. Requiring excellent drainage and part shade, it is difficult to grow on the humid east coast. Plants grafted onto stock of the Lemon-scented Myrtle, *Darwinia citriodora*, are hardier. Frost hardy. Propagate from cuttings.

Cranbrook Bell · *Darwinia meeboldii*   *Zones:* A G

This beautiful species is not easy to grow in the open ground but may be grown fairly readily in a container with a well-drained open soil mix. In these conditions it will reach about 1 m high by 60 cm across, with bell-shaped spring flowers with white and red outward-curving bracts. Frost hardy. Propagate from cuttings.

• **Wynyabbie Gem** *Westringia* 'Wynyabbie Gem'

• **Bundled Darwinia** *Darwinia fascicularis*

• **Cranbrook Bell** *Darwinia meeboldii*

• **Lemon-scented Myrtle** *Darwinia citriodora*

• **Stirlings Bell** *Darwinia lejostyla*

Mountain Devil

 The Mountain Devil belongs to the genus Lambertia, a member of the protea family. There are nine other related species all of which occur in Western Australia. The Mountain Devil, which occurs in New South Wales, is the easiest to grow.

Mountain Devil · *Lambertia formosa*   *Zones:* **A B C D**

So named for its strangely shaped fruits, which resemble an animal's face, this hardy shrub will reach 2 m high by 1.5 m across. The dark green leaves end in a sharp point and the flowers are borne in clusters at the ends of branchlets in spring and summer. They are surrounded by red bracts and birds appreciate their nectar. Most well-drained soils and full sun or part shade are suitable. Frost hardy. Propagate from seed or cuttings.

Mulla-mullas

 The genus Ptilotus is widespread throughout arid Australia, with about 90 species, many of them known as mulla-mullas or pussy-tails. Not many of them have been brought into cultivation, but recent research triggered by their value as cut flowers has resulted in at least two species now being available commercially.

Cotton Bush 'Ozlotus Pink Suantra' · *Ptilotus obovatus*   *Zones:* **H**

Although this cultivar has been specially developed for the cut-flower trade, it makes a handsome small shrub to 1 m high by 1.5 m across suitable for gardens in arid areas. The rounded, grey, felt-like leaves are about 4 cm long and the fluffy heads of pink and grey flowers are borne on branching stems for some months in spring and early summer. This plant does best in a sunny position in sandy soil. Frost tender.

Pink Mulla-mulla 'Ozlotus Abell Star' · *Ptilotus exaltatus*   *Zones:* **H**

Like 'Ozlotus Pink Suantra', this erect perennial has been developed as a cut flower and is being propagated by tissue culture. It has long narrow leaves to 20 cm and a flowering spike that rises to 60 cm, with a woolly head of lilac-grey flowers. It is seen for an extended period from late winter. It grows best in a sunny position in sandy well-drained soil. Frost tender.

• Mountain Devil *Lambertia formosa*

• Cotton Bush *Ptilotus obovatus*

• Pink Mulla-mulla *Ptilotus exaltatus*

Native Beeches

Although related to the deciduous true beeches of the Northern Hemisphere, the two species mentioned here are evergreen. A third species, native to the Tasmanian mountains, is one of our few native deciduous trees but has proved difficult in cultivation. The genus Nothofagus *is another with Gondwanan ancestry, having members on the east coast of Australia and also in Chile.*

Myrtle Beech • *Nothofagus cunninghamii*   Zones: A B C

While too large for most gardens, this slow-growing tree is ideal for a large property or can be used as an indoor plant in a container while it is small. The handsome leaves are more or less triangular, to about 2 cm long with toothed margins. The flowers and fruits are insignificant. Available from Tasmanian nurseries, it requires a well-composted loamy soil and ample moisture. Although it will stand full sun it prefers shade. Frost hardy. Propagation is from seed.

Antarctic Beech • *Nothofagus moorei*   Zones: A B C D

This tall tree from highland rainforests of New South Wales and southern Queensland has brown scaly bark and shiny dark green leaves with toothed margins. The young growth is reddish. Like Myrtle Beech, it may be used as an indoor plant when young. It requires a well-composted, loamy soil in sun or shade. Frost hardy. Propagate from seed.

Native Bluebell

The species described here is a perennial herb, a member of a large genus with about 200 species that includes about 20 species native to Australia. Most are not available commercially. The following species is frequently seen in nurseries and is easy to grow.

Native Bluebell • *Wahlenbergia stricta*   Zones: A B C D G H

The most commonly grown native bluebell is this one, which forms a clump about 40 cm high with masses of light blue star-shaped flowers, about 2 cm in diameter, borne in spring and summer. It will accept most soils but likes a sunny situation. Unlike the European Bluebell, it is not a bulb, but an evergreen herb with a fibrous root system. Frost hardy. Propagate from seed.

• Myrtle Beech *Nothofagus cunninghamii*

• Antarctic Beech *Nothofagus moorei*

• Native Bluebell *Wahlenbergia stricta*

Native Irises

 There a number of native genera in the iris family but the true irises do not occur naturally in Australia. The plants described below have similar flowers, however, with three petals and three sepals, and form tufted plants with narrow sword-shaped leaves.

White Iris · *Diplarrena moraea*   *Zones:* A B C D G

This tufted plant with strap-shaped leaves to 40 cm bears white spring and summer flowers with a yellow centre on stems a little longer than the leaves. Sepals and petals are similar. It is hardy in most soils and aspects and looks particularly attractive near a pool feature. Frost hardy. Propagate from seed or by division.

Branching Grass Flag · *Libertia paniculata*   *Zones:* A B C D G

This tufted perennial has grass-like leaves to 50 cm long and a branching stem of white flowers to 40 cm tall in spring. It is hardy in most soils but prefers ample moisture and some shade. Frost hardy. Propagate by seed or by division.

Purple Flag · *Patersonia sericea*   *Zones:* A B C D G

This tufted plant has strap-like leaves to 40 cm and purple flowers borne on a stem a little shorter than the leaves. While the flowers are fragile and last only a few hours, they are produced over a long period in spring and make a worthwhile display. Each flower is about 5 cm across, with the three sepals being prominent. A well-drained soil and a sunny position are recommended. Frost hardy. Propagate from seed.

Western Purple Flag · *Patersonia occidentalis*   *Zones:* A B C D G

While similar in most respects to the Purple Flag, this plant is generally more robust, with leaves to 40 cm and a flower spike to 80 cm in spring. The flowers are purple. Good drainage is particularly important and the plant requires full sun. Frost hardy. Propagate from seed.

Yellow Flag · *Patersonia umbrosa* var. *xanthina*   *Zones:* A C G

While all other *Patersonia* species have purplish flowers, this one is brilliant yellow. It forms an erect clump with stiff narrow leaves to 50 cm long and a spike of spring flowers to about the same length. Again, while the flowers are short lived, many flowers are produced over a long period. Excellent drainage is important and full sun or a little shade are suitable. Frost hardy. Propagate from seed.

• Branching Grass Flag *Libertia paniculata*

• White Iris *Diplarrena moraea*

• Purple Flag *Patersonia sericea*

• Western Purple Flag *Patersonia occidentalis*

• Yellow Flag *Patersonia umbrosa* var. *xanthina*

Native Pines (Conifers)

Conifers are not as common in the Australian flora as in the Northern Hemisphere flora. However, most of the roughly 44 native species are useful plants for gardens and parks. Conifers do not produce flowers, their seeds being held in cones, and male and female cones are often formed on separate plants.

Australian Kauri · *Agathis robusta*   Zones: B D E F

This tall tree to 30 m is too large for the average garden but is excellent for larger properties and parks. It may also be used as a container plant when young. The leaves are large for a conifer, being more or less oval and about 10 cm long. The cones are about 12 cm long. Most loamy soils are suitable and it will accept full sun. It may not tolerate heavy frosts. Propagate from seed.

Norfolk Island Pine · *Araucaria heterophylla*   Zones: B D E F G

Ideal for beachside plantings, this handsome tree to 25 m is resistant to salt spray. It is too large for the average suburban garden but may be used as an indoor plant, its horizontal branches making it particularly suitable as a Christmas tree. Most soils and aspects are suitable. It is not tolerant of heavy frosts. Propagate from seed.

King Billy Pine · *Athrotaxis selaginoides*   Zones: A C

This Tasmanian tree is very slow growing and makes an excellent container plant. In the open ground it may eventually reach 40 m in ideal conditions but this would take many years. Its bright green foliage is a feature and it produces small spherical cones about 2 cm in diameter. Most soils and aspects are suitable but it will only grow well in cool temperate climates. Frost hardy. Propagate from cuttings.

Cypress Pine · *Callitris columellaris*   Zones: A B D

Members of the genus *Callitris* bear male and female cones on the one tree. This more or less columnar tree to 10 m in height has fine dark green foliage; the small, globular female cones are about 2 cm in diameter. It would suit a formal garden and tolerates most soils and aspects. Frost hardy. Propagate from seed.

White Cypress Pine · *Callitris glaucophylla*   Zones: A B C D G H

A little taller than the Cypress Pine, *Callitris columellaris*, and with blue-grey foliage, this species is also suitable for a formal garden. The female cones are up to 2.5 cm in diameter. Most soils and aspects are suitable, and it is resistant to extended dry periods. Frost hardy. Propagate from seed.

• **Australian Kauri** *Agathis robusta*

• **King Billy Pine** *Athrotaxis selaginoides*

• **Cypress Pine** *Callitris columellaris*

• **Norfolk Island Pine** *Araucaria heterophylla*

• **White Cypress Pine** *Callitris glaucophylla*

Port Jackson Pine · *Callitris rhomboidea*　　　　*Zones:* A B C D G H

Rather like a pencil pine in habit, this narrow columnar tree will reach 15 m in height. The new growth at the apex of the tree tends to be pendulous. The female cones tend to be clustered together. Most soils and aspects are suitable but this tree does best where ample moisture is available. Frost hardy. Propagate from seed.

Mallee Pine · *Callitris verrucosa*　　　　*Zones:* A C G H

Suited to arid and semi-arid areas, this tree rarely exceeds 6 m in height by about 4 m across. It has a less formal appearance than the other three *Callitris* species listed here. The foliage is greyish and the female cones, about 2.5 cm in diameter, are covered with wart-like tubercles. Prefers full sun and a well-drained soil. Frost hardy. Propagate from seed.

Brown Pine · *Podocarpus elatus*　　　　*Zones:* A B C D E G

Podocarpus species have male and female cones on separate trees. This is a medium-sized tree with a spreading crown and narrow oblong leaves to 17 cm with a sharp point. The female cones are succulent, bluish black and edible, about 2.5 cm in diameter. This tree is common in cultivation and is often used as a street tree, although it is slow growing. It also makes a good container plant. Most soils and aspects are suitable. Frost hardy. Propagate from seed or cuttings.

Spiny Plum Pine · *Podocarpus spinulosus*　　　　*Zones:* A B C D G

This species forms an erect to spreading shrub up to 2 m in height with shiny narrow leaves to 6 cm long with pointed tips. The blue-black, succulent, female cones are about 1 cm in diameter. The shrub forms a useful low screen. It is hardy in most soils and aspects and will tolerate salty winds. Frost hardy. Propagate from cuttings.

Tropical Plum Pine · *Podocarpus grayae*　　　　*Zones:* D E

This medium-sized tree eventually reaches 6–7 m in height, with shiny, narrow leaves to 25 cm long that tend to hang down from the branches. The succulent female cones are red. It is a slow-growing species, making a wonderful feature plant in the garden or a fine container plant. Most soils are suitable and the plant will tolerate full sun or part shade. Probably frost tender. Propagate from cuttings or seed.

Mountain Plum Pine · *Podocarpus lawrencei*　　　　*Zones:* A B C D

This variable plant may form a low scrambling shrub or a small tree to 8 m depending on the origin of the clone. It has grey-green oblong leaves about 1.5 cm long and red succulent female cones. Although alpine in origin, this species will grow well in the subtropics. It also makes a good tub plant. Most soils and aspects are suitable. Propagate from cuttings.

• Port Jackson Pine *Callitris rhomboidea*

• Mallee Pine *Callitris verrucosa*

• Brown Pine *Podocarpus elatus*

• Spiny Plum Pine *Podocarpus spinulosus*

• Tropical Plum Pine *Podocarpus grayae*

• Mountain Plum Pine *Podocarpus lawrencei*

Mt Spurgeon Black Pine · *Prumnopitys ladei*   *Zones:* B D E

A narrow columnar tree of medium size, Mt Spurgeon Black Pine has dark green oblong leaves to 1.5 cm long arranged in two rows on opposite sides of the stems. It is very slow growing and suitable both for garden use and as a container plant for indoors or on a patio. The succulent female cones are bluish black. It will accept most soils and aspects, but is probably frost tender. Propagate from cuttings, which take some months to form roots.

Net Bushes or One-sided Bottlebrushes

 The genus Calothamnus *is restricted in the wild to Western Australia but has proved adaptable to cultivation on the east coast also. Most species have red flowers and tend to flower on the old wood. The individual flowers are clustered together, mostly on one side of the stem, giving rise to the common name 'one-sided bottlebrush'. Honeyeaters enjoy their nectar.*

Common Net Bush · *Calothamnus quadrifidus*   *Zones:* A B G H

This erect or slightly spreading shrub will reach 2.5 m high by 2.5 m across, with pine-like foliage to 3 cm in length. The red or, rarely, yellow flowers are borne in long spikes to 10 cm in spring, summer and autumn. It prefers a well-drained soil in full sun. Slightly frost tender. Propagate from seed.

Mouse Ears · *Calothamnus rupestris*   *Zones:* A G H

The strange common name of this plant relates to the odd appearance of the large woody fruits, which have two prominent lobes that resemble ears. Probably the most beautiful of the genus, this rounded shrub reaches 2 m in height. The slender pine-like leaves are about 3 cm long and the pink to rose red flowers, about 4 cm long, are borne in clusters on the old wood in spring. Excellent drainage and a little shade are recommended. Frost hardy. Propagate from seed.

Broad-leaved Net Bush · *Calothamnus homalophyllus*   *Zones:* A B C G

This hardy species will reach 2 m high by 2 m across and may have red or yellow flowers in one-sided spikes on the old wood. Prefers full sun and reasonably well-drained soils. It is tolerant to all but the hardest frosts. Propagate from seed.

• Mt Spurgeon Black Pine *Prumnopitys ladei*

• **Common Net Bush** *Calothamnus quadrifidus*

• Mouse Ears *Calothamnus rupestris*

• **Broad-leaved Net Bush** *Calothamnus homalophyllus*

Orchids

Australia has about 700 species of native orchids. Some are small and insignificant plants; others have large, showy flowers. Many native orchids grow in the ground and are often quite difficult to cultivate; they are best left to experts. The more common species in cultivation are epiphytes, which grow naturally on trees or rocks and are generally easier to grow. Many epiphytes have thick stems known as pseudobulbs which can absorb water and nutrients. Propagation from seed is complex; some may be propagated by division.

Native Cymbidium • *Cymbidium madidum*   *Zones:* B D E F

Australia has three native *Cymbidium* orchids and this one is the easiest to grow. It has been hybridised with exotic species to produce cultivars with smaller flowers than the exotic varieties. It is a large plant with long leaves to 90 cm and robust pseudobulbs. The pendulous flower spike is up to 8 cm long with green or brownish flowers about 3 cm in diameter, opening in spring. It is best cultivated in an open potting mixture designed for exotic cymbidiums or grown in a hollow log in open compost. Grow in semi-shade or in a shade house. Frost tender. If old pseudobulbs are removed and placed in compost, they will send out shoots — the new plants may be cut away and planted out.

Cooktown Orchid • *Dendrobium phalaenopsis*   *Zones:* E F

The floral emblem of Queensland, this beautiful orchid must be grown in a heated glasshouse wherever temperatures fall below 15°C. The plant produces long canes to 30 cm or more, with several green leaves at the top. The spring flower spike emerges from near the top of the cane with several large purple flowers about 6 cm in diameter. It may be potted in large pine-bark pieces or tied to a solid log of cork bark or hardwood. In the tropics it may be tied tightly to a tree with permanent bark. Ample light and daily water.

Pink Rock Orchid • *Dendrobium kingianum*   *Zones:* B D E F

This diminutive orchid grows naturally on rocks. It has short pseudobulbs to 20 cm, often less, with several dark green leaves at the apex. Prolific spring flowers vary in colour from white to deep pink or mauve and are about 2 cm in diameter. Grow in pots in an open mix of pine bark or attached to rocks in an open position with good light. Frost tender.

Rock Orchid • *Dendrobium speciosum*   *Zones:* B D E F

Two forms of this hardy orchid are available. One has short pseudobulbs to 30 cm long and mostly occurs naturally on rocks. It has cream spring flowers on spikes to 45 cm. The other has pseudobulbs to 70 cm long and tends to grow naturally on trees. It has white flowers in even longer sprays than the former. Both may be grown on rocks or in an open compost in the garden in mild climates. Good light is essential for good flowering. Frost tender.

• Native Cymbidium *Cymbidium madidum*

• Cooktown Orchid *Dendrobium phalaenopsis*

• Pink Rock Orchid *Dendrobium kingianum*

• Rock Orchid *Dendrobium speciosum*

Nodding Greenhood · *Pterostylis nutans*   *Zones:* A B C D G

Greenhoods are the easiest of the terrestrial orchids to cultivate. This species forms colonies of many hundreds of rosettes of soft green leaves; from the centre of each rosette a small flower stem rises to about 15 cm with a single green flower at the top. Small round tubers may be purchased from specialist native orchid growers. Grow in pots using an open mix containing some well-rotted compost. Keep reasonably dry until about autumn when new shoots will appear. Water more while the plants are growing and flowering, and less when they start to go dormant. Three or four tubers in a 120 mm squat pot will eventually make an attractive display. Keep in a shady position in a bush house. Frost hardy.

Orange Blossom Orchid · *Sarcochilus falcatus*   *Zones:* B D E

This epiphytic species is best grown on blocks of hardwood or cork bark. It does not produce a pseudobulb but three to eight broad, curving leaves to 15 cm long emerge from the base of the plant. Thick succulent roots cling to the log to secure the plant in position. The fragrant white spring flowers are about 3 cm in diameter. Grow in a shaded bushhouse and water daily. Tolerant of all but heavy frosts.

Palm Lilies

 The genus Cordyline *has about 20 species in the tropics and sub-tropics, with eight occurring in Australia. Although commonly known as palm lilies, they are not particularly palm-like or lily-like. They are many-stemmed, evergreen plants, very useful for low-light garden situations and as pot plants. Their unique form and colourful fruits make them ideal feature plants for shaded gardens, and they can be used indoors for extended periods.*

Broad-leaved Palm Lily · *Cordyline petiolaris*   *Zones:* B D E F

This tall plant reaches 5 m with several stems rising from the base. The leaves may reach 1 m long and about 12 cm at the widest point. The lower parts of the stems become bare. A branching spray of white spring flowers is followed by strings of bright red bead-like fruits. A well-composted soil in a shady position is required. Container plants may be brought inside for extended periods. Frost tender. Propagate from seed.

Narrow-leaved Palm Lily · *Cordyline stricta*   *Zones:* B D E F

Reaching 3 m in height, this palm-like plant develops many stems with narrow leaves to 50 cm long and 2 cm wide. The flowers, borne on branching sprays in spring and summer, are purplish and are followed by small, shiny black fruits. A well-composted soil in light or heavy shade is preferred. Like the previous species, it makes a worthwhile container plant. Frost tender. Propagate from seed.

• Nodding Greenhood *Pterostylis nutans*

• Orange Blossom Orchid *Sarcochilus falcatus*

• Broad-leaved Palm Lily *Cordyline petiolaris*

• Narrow-leaved Palm Lily *Cordyline stricta*

Palms and Cycads

Palms and cycads are treated together here as their uses in the garden are similar, although botanically they are very different. Australia has about 70 species of cycads, which are ancient plants in terms of their evolutionary development. They do not produce flowers and their seeds are formed from cones on female plants. Palms, on the other hand, are flowering plants, although their flowers are often not particularly ornamental. Both groups of plants have attractive form and foliage and their use in horticulture relies on these features.

Alexander Palm · *Archontophoenix alexandrae*   Zones: B D E F
A single-stemmed species, this palm grows to 13 m in height with fronds 3–4 m long, grey on the underside, that fall to the ground when they die. The white winter flowers are produced in branching pendulous sprays and are followed by red globular fruits. This palm grows quickly and is excellent for use in tropical and subtropical gardens. Most soils are suitable and full sun is tolerated. Native pigeons, particularly the beautiful Wampoo Pigeon, are attracted to the fruits. Frost tender. Propagate from seed.

Cabbage Tree Palm · *Livistona australis*   Zones: A B D E
This tall palm reaches 25 m in height and is Australia's most cold-tolerant species. The fronds are fan-shaped, bright green and up to 4 m long. Small white flowers are produced in large sprays amongst the leaves in winter. Most soils are suitable. Tolerates full sun. Susceptible to heavy frost. Propagate from seed.

Native Fan Palm · *Licuala ramsayi*   Zones: B D E F
A slow-growing species, this palm eventually reaches about 10 m in height, with huge circular fronds 1.5 m in diameter that often split as they age. Although native to north Queensland, it will grow in frost-free areas as far south as Sydney. This makes a wonderful feature plant if it is given a well-composted soil and part to full shade. The flowers are insignificant. Frost tender. Propagate from seed.

Walking Stick Palm · *Linospadix monostachya*   Zones: B D E
This slender dwarf palm rarely exceeds 3 m in height, with fronds that are up to 1.2 m long. The small cream flowers are carried on an unbranched stem and are followed by bright red globular fruits in autumn. It is an excellent palm for a small shady garden. It is very slow to start but once a trunk is formed growth accelerates. Grow in a well-composted soil. Frost tender. Propagate from seed.

• **Alexander Palm** *Archontophoenix alexandrae*

• **Cabbage Tree Palm** *Livistona australis*

• **Native Fan Palm** *Licuala ramsayi*

• **Walking Stick Palm** *Linospadix monostachya*

Burrawang • *Macrozamia communis*   *Zones:* A B D

Producing only a short trunk, this common cycad has fronds to 1.5 m long. The barrel-shaped female cones develop bright red seeds on maturity. Male cones are more slender. It makes a useful tub plant. Hardy in most soils and tolerates full sun or part shade. Susceptible to heavy frosts. The seeds are poisonous, but Aborigines ate them after carefully treating them to remove the toxins. Propagate from seed.

Zamia Palm • *Cycas media*   *Zones:* B D E F G H

Developing a thickened trunk to 3 m high by 20 cm in diameter, this cycad produces many bright green fronds to 1.5 m long. The male cone is ovoid and about 20 cm long. It collapses once its pollen has been released. The female cone is rounded with many golf ball-sized brown fruits forming a skirt around the top of the trunk. It will grow in most soils but like most cycads is very slow growing and will not form a trunk for several years. It makes a good container plant. Full sun and part shade are both tolerated. Slightly frost tender. Propagate from seed.

Pineapple Zamia • *Lepidozamia peroffskyana*   *Zones:* B D E

This handsome cycad has shiny dark green fronds to 2.5 m long and develops huge female cones resembling enormous brownish pineapples, 70 cm long by 30 cm wide. The male cones are much narrower. It will produce its first fruit in about 10–12 years from seed. The robust trunk takes many years to form. Grow in a well-composted loamy soil in half shade. It is a good container plant. Slightly frost tender. Propagate from seed.

Pandanus

Pandanus, or screw pines as they are sometimes called, occur around the subtropical and tropical coasts and rivers of Australia. Several species are also found in tropical rainforests.

Pandanus • *Pandanus tectorius* var. *australianus*   *Zones:* B D E F

This is the most common species and possibly the only one available commercially. It is a small spreading tree with many thick prop-roots that support it against the salt-laden winds of its natural coastal environment. The spirally arranged leaves are up to 1 m long with many sharp spines along their margins and mid-rib. The fruits on female trees look like large pineapples and are orange when ripe. This species will grow in most soils but full sun is recommended. The root system may become invasive in good soils. Its unique appearance may provide a feature in warm climate gardens. Frost tender. Propagate from seed.

• **Burrawang** *Macrozamia communis*

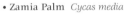

• **Zamia Palm** *Cycas media*

• **Pineapple Zamia** *Lepidozamia peroffskyana*

• **Pandanus** *Pandanus tectorius* var. *australianus*

Pea Flowers

 Pea flowers are an important element of the Australian bush on both sides of the continent, particularly in the heath and dry sclerophyll forest environments. Many have yellow flowers that light up the spring flowering display. Some are a little touchy to cultivate but the species mentioned below are hardy in the climatic zones recommended. They all need to be propagated from seed which has been soaked in boiling water overnight.

Leafless Pea · *Bossiaea scolopendria*
Zones: A B C D G

An erect, sparsely branched shrub to 1 m high, the Leafless Pea is so named for the flattened stems that act as leaves. The yellow and brown pea flowers are borne along the stems in spring. This unusual species may be a feature in a rockery. It requires excellent drainage. Probably does best in a little shade, although it will tolerate full sun. Frost hardy.

Flame Pea · *Chorizema cordatum*
Zones: A B C G

An erect or spreading shrub to 1 m or a little less, the Flame Pea has broad leaves about 6 cm long with toothed margins. Its sprays of red flowers are produced prolifically in spring. Prune lightly after flowering to improve its shape. Good drainage and full or half sun are required, and a well-mulched soil is an advantage. Susceptible to heavy frosts.

Heathy Parrot Pea · *Dillwynia retorta*
Zones: A B C D G

The most common form of this species forms a shrub to 1.5 m by 1 m across, but prostrate forms are sometimes found in nurseries. It has slightly twisted heath-like leaves to 1 cm long and yellow and reddish-brown pea flowers in spring. A well-drained sandy soil in full or part sun is recommended. Prune lightly after flowering. Frost hardy.

Hovea · *Hovea acutifolia*
Zones: B D

This species forms an erect plant to 1.5 m high by 1 m across. The narrow elliptical leaves are about 8 cm long and the prolific purple pea flowers are borne prolifically in late winter and spring. Prune after flowering. Ample water is required, but good drainage is also important. Grow in light shade. Probably frost tender.

Austral Indigo · *Indigofera australis*
Zones: A B C D G H

Variable in size, this species may form an erect sparsely branched shrub to 1 m or a more robust, spreading shrub to 2 m by 2 m. Check on the nursery label when purchasing a plant. The foliage is bluish green and the purple or, rarely, white pea flowers appear in spring. This hardy species will grow in most soils and aspects. Frost hardy.

• **Leafless Pea** *Bossiaea scolopendria*

• **Flame Pea** *Chorizema cordatum*

• **Heathy Parrot Pea** *Dillwynia retorta*

• **Austral Indigo** *Indigofera australis*

• **Hovea** *Hovea acutifolia*

Prostrate Shaggy Pea · *Podolobium scandens*

Zones: B D

This prostrate species has elliptical dark green leaves to 5 cm long and orange pea flowers in spring. It is an excellent ground cover when planted 70 cm apart. Plant in loamy soils with reasonable drainage; prefers full sun for best flowering. Possibly frost tender. It is tolerant of salt-laden winds. Propagate from seed or from cuttings.

Forest Bush Pea or Bacon and Eggs · *Pultenaea villosa*

Zones: A B C D

A small shrub to about 1 m high with pendulous branches and small hairy leaves, this plant flowers prolifically in spring with yellow and brown pea flowers. The common name Bacon and Eggs has been applied to many of our pea flowers with yellow and brown flowers. This hardy species will accept most soils and full sun or part shade. Its weeping habit is a feature. Frost hardy. Propagate from seed or from cuttings.

Darling Pea · *Swainsona galegifolia*

Zones: A B C G H

This plant is a perennial with soft branches rising to 80 cm in height to form its crown. The large pea flowers are borne in sprays in spring with the flower colour varying from white through pinks to mauve and even red. When flowering is finished, the plants should be cut back in winter to near the base to make room for the new growth which will bear flowers the next season. Most soils and full sun are recommended. This species is both drought and frost tolerant.

Sturt's Desert Pea · *Swainsona formosa*

Zones: H

This beautiful plant is not easy to grow anywhere but in arid or semi-arid areas. It is prostrate with hairy grey-green leaves and wonderful large showy pea flowers in spring, which are typically red with a black centre or more rarely white, pink or all red. The stems will spread to about 1 m long. This species is best treated as an annual; sow the seed in late winter in very well-drained sandy soil and full sun. Keep moist until germination occurs. Frost tender. Seed is sometimes available in commercial packets.

• Prostrate Shaggy Pea *Podolobium scandens*

• Forest Bush Pea or Bacon and Eggs *Pultenaea villosa*

• Darling Pea *Swainsona galegifolia*

• Sturt's Desert Pea *Swainsona formosa*

Pelargoniums

About 250 species of Pelargonium *are scattered across the warm areas of the world. Australia has six native species, with several exotics having become naturalised from garden escapees.*

Austral Storksbill • *Pelargonium australe*
Zones: **A** B C D **G** H

Most plants of this species form a rounded bush about 50 cm in diameter with rounded lobed leaves. Spring and summer flowers in sprays of 4 –12 blooms, each about 1.5 cm in diameter, may be almost white with purple veins to mauve. Most soils are suitable. Flowers best in full sun. Frost hardy. Propagate from cuttings, which strike very readily.

Magenta Storksbill • *Pelargonium rodneyanum*
Zones: **A** B C D **G** H

This stemless plant develops a carrot-like root, which allows it to store water and nutrients. The broad leaves are up to 5 cm long and the slender stalks of magenta spring flowers are about 20 cm long. The whole plant is less than 30 cm high. This is an excellent rockery plant with neat foliage and colourful flowers. Most reasonably well-drained soils are suitable. Tolerates full sun or part shade. Frost hardy. Propagate from seed.

Pigface

The common garden pigface is native to South Africa. Australia has several species that belong to the same family and inhabit areas where their succulent leaves help them to survive harsh natural environments, both in arid areas and on exposed coastal dunes and headlands.

Pigface • *Carpobrotus glaucescens*
Zones: **A** B D **G**

This prostrate plant has thick succulent leaves to 10 cm long that are triangular in cross section. Large purple flowers with white centres, about 6 cm in diameter, are produced throughout the year. Best suited to dry sandy sites in full sun, this plant is resistant to salt spray and is sometimes used to stabilise sand dunes. Frost tender. Propagate from cuttings.

Rounded Noon Flower •
Disphyma crassifolium ssp. *clavellatum*
Zones: **A** B C **G** H

A prostrate creeping plant, this species is ideal for coastal sites or inland sites where saline soils are encountered. The succulent leaves are more or less egg-shaped and about 4 cm long. Purple flowers, about 3 cm in diameter, are seen for most of the year. Most soils are satisfactory and full sun is recommended. Resistant to light frosts. Propagate from cuttings.

• **Austral Storksbill** *Pelargonium australe*

• **Magenta Storksbill** *Pelargonium rodneyanum*

• **Pigface** *Carpobrotus glaucescens*

• **Rounded Noon Flower** *Disphyma crassifolium* ssp. *clavellatum*

Rainforest Trees and Shrubs

 The use of rainforest plants has become popular in recent years as we learn more about these plants and their cultivation requirements. Many plants from this environment are trees far too big for the average home garden, but the selection given here includes some smaller plants that would enhance most suburban blocks and are readily available. In general, rainforest plants require a rich well-composted soil which is mulched with leaf litter or similar material. They will thrive with generous applications of general fertiliser; give them ample water during dry periods. Most will tolerate shade but will also accept full sun. Many may also be used as indoor plants when young.

Tree Waratah • *Alloxylon flammeum*
Zones: B D E

A medium-sized tree to 10 m high with shiny leaves to 18 cm long, this species has bright red flowers borne in large clusters near the branch ends. They appear in spring. It makes a wonderful specimen tree suitable for larger gardens in frost-free areas as far south as Sydney. Prefers reasonable drainage. Propagate from seed or preferably from cuttings, which provide flowers earlier.

Rose Myrtle • *Archirhodomyrtus beckleri*
Zones: B D E

This spring-flowering large shrub or sometimes small tree will reach about 6 m in height with glossy light green leaves to 8 cm long. The pink five-petalled flowers are fragrant and about 8 cm in diameter. They are followed by small orange berries, which birds enjoy. It is suitable for small gardens. Full sun or part shade in a well-mulched soil give the best results. Slightly frost tender. Propagate from seed.

Atherton Oak • *Athertonia diversifolia*
Zones: D E F

Too large for most suburban gardens, this handsome tree reaches 25 m high and has large juvenile leaves that resemble enormous oak leaves. As the tree ages the leaf shape changes to a simple, dark green, shiny leaf about 30 cm long. The drooping flower spike, about 25 cm long, bears white and brown flowers in autumn and winter that are followed by blue edible fruits. It is an excellent foliage plant for frost-free areas. Propagate from seed.

Austromyrtus • *Austromyrtus inophloia*
Zones: D E F

This bushy shrub may reach 5 m in height but is usually smaller. The small leaves are 5 cm long and the young tips are reddish. The cultivar 'Aurora' has rich burgundy young growth. White flowers about 8 mm in diameter are seen in spring. While this species may be used in the garden, it also makes a great tub plant for the patio. The new growth is spectacular. Frost tender. Propagate from cuttings.

• Tree Waratah *Alloxylon flammeum*

• Rose Myrtle *Archirhodomyrtus beckleri*

• Atherton Oak *Athertonia diversifolia*

• Austromyrtus *Austromyrtus inophloia*

Lemon Myrtle · *Backhousia citriodora*   Zones: B D E F

Grown commercially for its aromatic foliage, from which a food flavouring is extracted, this medium-sized tree to 15 m high is also a useful ornamental. The foliage is lemon-scented and in February the tree is covered with fluffy cream flowers, which retain their calyces after the petals fall and thus extend the period of interest. This tree will sucker in good soils. Frost tender. Propagate from cuttings.

Ivory Curl Flower · *Buckinghamia celsissima*   Zones: A B D E F

This medium-sized bushy tree rarely exceeds 15 m in cultivation and usually has branches to the ground. The large, shiny, dark green leaves are about 15 cm long. It has prolific spikes of creamy white flowers in summer and autumn, depending on the location, and flowers well as far south as Melbourne. Probably frost tender. Propagate from seed or cuttings.

Black Bean · *Castanospermum australe*   Zones: B D E F

This large tree to 40 m high is too big for the average garden but may be used when young as a container plant indoors. The shiny compound leaves are about 30 cm long. Red and yellow pea flowers are produced in spring on the old wood of mature trees. These are followed by large boat-shaped seed pods. Frost tender. Propagate from seed, which was eaten by the Aborigines only after careful preparation to leach out the poisonous alkaloids.

Tuckeroo · *Cupaniopsis anacardioides*   Zones: A B D E F

This small densely foliaged tree may reach 10 m high. It is resistant to salty winds and is a favourite for use near the sea to provide shelter for more sensitive plants. It has shiny compound leaves and small autumn insignificant flowers followed by sprays of orange fruits about 1 cm in diameter. It grows well as far south as Melbourne but is probably sensitive to heavy frosts. Propagate from seed.

Blueberry Ash 'Prima Donna' ·
Elaeocarpus reticulatus 'Prima Donna'   Zones: A B D E

The lance-shaped toothed leaves of this hardy small tree to 10 m are about 12 cm long and in spring the tree produces masses of fringed bell-shaped flowers. White is the normal colour but the pink-flowered cultivar 'Prima Donna' is preferred. Satin Bower Birds enjoy the blue globular fruits that follow the flowers. This plant is relatively slow growing and makes an excellent plant for a large tub. Requires ample water and well-composted and well-drained soil. Frost hardy. Propagate from cuttings.

Native Teak · *Flindersia australis*   Zones: D E

This very large tree to 40 m high is best suited for large properties or parks where it makes a wonderful shade tree with a rounded canopy. The dark green compound leaves have 3–13 elliptical leaflets and at maturity large sprays of small white flowers cover the tree in spring. The fruits are large and when ripe open into five segments with a roughened reverse. They are often used in floral arrangements. Frost tender. Propagate from fresh seed.

• Lemon Myrtle *Backhousia citriodora*

• Ivory Curl Flower *Buckinghamia celsissima*

• Black Bean *Castanospermum australe*

• Tuckeroo *Cupaniopsis anacardioides*

• Blueberry Ash 'Prima Donna' *Elaeocarpus reticulatus* 'Prima Donna'

• Native Teak *Flindersia australis*

Tulipwood · *Harpullia pendula*   *Zones:* B D E

This medium-sized tree to 20 m high forms a spreading canopy and is an excellent shade tree. The compound leaves are shiny and the yellowish summer flowers are about 12 mm in diameter. These are followed by two-lobed fruits, which may be red or yellow, with two glossy black seeds exposed at maturity. It is often used as a street tree in mild to warm climates and is suited to larger gardens. Sensitive to heavy frosts. Propagate from seed.

Brush Box · *Lophostemon confertus*   *Zones:* A B D

This tall tree to 35 m high is best used in parks and large properties. Its brown bark and whorled dark green leaves make it a handsome shade tree. The white feathery spring flowers are not particularly obvious. Reasonably frost hardy. Propagate from seed.

Macadamia Nut · *Macadamia tetraphylla*   *Zones:* B D G

This well-known medium-sized tree to 20 m high is used commercially for its flavoursome nuts. It can also be grown in gardens where it forms an attractive tree and will also produce nuts. The narrow leathery leaves may have toothed edges. Flowers are borne in spring in pendulous sprays and may be creamy white or purplish. Nuts are produced from February to May, depending on variety and location. Hardy to mild frosts. May be grown from seed but grafted plants developed to ensure good nut production are preferable.

Umbrella Tree · *Schefflera actinophylla*   *Zones:* B D E F G

Umbrella trees are frequently grown as indoor plants but they also make good garden plants in mild or warm climates. This species forms a many-trunked tree to 10 m in height with light green, glossy, umbrella-like leaves, the elliptical leaflets radiating from a central point. A branching spray of red flowers is borne at the apex of the trunks in winter. Birds are attracted to the fruits, causing the species to be spread into areas where it is not native. Best not to grow near bushland. Frost tender. Propagate from cuttings.

Firewheel Tree · *Stenocarpus sinuatus*   *Zones:* A B D G

This beautiful tree with its shiny, often lobed leaves usually does not exceed 10 m in cultivation although it may be taller in the forest. Its showy red flowers are formed in the shape of cartwheels and make a fine display in February and March. It is slow growing for the first few years and takes about five or six years to flower. Tolerant of light frosts. Propagate from seed.

Banana Bush · *Tabernaemontana pandacaqui*   *Zones:* B D E

This spreading open shrub will reach 2.5 m in a well-shaded spot in the garden. Its lance-shaped leaves are up to 10 cm long and its fragrant white spring flowers, 1.5 cm in diameter, resemble a propeller. They are followed in summer by inedible banana-shaped yellow fruits about 4 cm long containing red seeds. Frost tender. Propagate from seed.

• Tulipwood *Harpullia pendula*

• Brush Box *Lophostemon confertus*

• Macadamia Nut *Macadamia tetraphylla*

• Umbrella Tree *Schefflera actinophylla*

• Firewheel Tree *Stenocarpus sinuatus*

• Banana Bush *Tabernaemontana pandacaqui*

Water Gum · *Tristaniopsis laurina*   *Zones:* **A** B C D **G**

This small tree to 8 m high has narrow glossy leaves to 10 cm long and makes a good shade tree for the small garden. Its fawn bark is attractive and the small yellow flowers are well displayed in summer. In cold climates the leaves tend to redden. It also makes an excellent street tree. Frost hardy. Propagate from seed.

Weeping Satin Ash · *Waterhousea floribunda*   *Zones:* **A** B D

This very fast-growing tree may be a little large for most suburban gardens but will provide an excellent screen in the appropriate position. In ideal conditions it will reach 15m high. Its shiny dark green leaves and pendulous branches are features. Small, fluffy, white summer flowers are followed by greenish fruits. Tolerant of mild frosts. Propagate from seed.

Golden Penda · *Xanthostemon chrysanthus*   *Zones:* B D **E**

This medium-sized tree to 15 m high has glossy, dark green, lance-shaped leaves to 18 cm long with red young growth. Large fluffy yellow flowers are produced in winter. This is a feature tree and although moderately tall can be accommodated in most gardens. Most nursery-grown plants are produced from cuttings; these tend to be bushy to the ground and will flower in the first season. Frost tender. Propagate from cuttings.

Note: Some of the most lovely and easy-to-grow rainforest plants are the lilly pillies, which are so numerous as to deserve a separate listing starting on page 90.

Rhododendron

Australia has only two native rhododendrons, both of which are found on several high peaks of north Queensland. They are very similar but the one described here is more readily available commercially.

Native Rhododendron · *Rhododendron lochiae*   *Zones:* **A** B D **E**

This species forms a rounded bush about 80 cm high with shiny broad leaves and red trumpet-shaped flowers about 5 cm in diameter at their mouth. They appear in spring and summer. This plant requires an open, well-composted, slightly acid soil and very good drainage. Half shade is ideal. It makes an excellent tub plant that may be brought indoors when flowering. Will tolerate mild frosts. Propagate from cuttings.

• **Water Gum** *Tristaniopsis laurina*

• **Weeping Satin Ash** *Waterhousea floribunda*

• **Golden Penda** *Xanthostemon chrysanthus*

• **Native Rhododendron** *Rhododendron lochiae*

Rice Flowers

Members of the genus Pimelea *are known as rice flowers. The reason for this common name is uncertain. Possibly it refers to the seed, which is a little like a rice grain. There are over 100 species in the genus; most are native. Many are still rare in cultivation and some have proved difficult to maintain in gardens. Those given here are relatively easy, if good drainage is provided.*

Pink Rice Flower • *Pimelea ferruginea*   *Zones:* A B C G
This neat rounded shrub to 1 m high, with shiny oval leaves 1–2 cm long, produces a profusion of pink flowerheads about 3 cm in diameter in spring. Flower colour varies considerably, from very pale to deep pink; several named cultivars are available. Excellent drainage is essential and flowering is best in full sun. Frost hardy. Propagate from cuttings.

Slender Rice Flower • *Pimelea linifolia*   *Zones:* A B C D G
This variable small shrub may be erect and sparsely branched to 50 cm high or compact and almost prostrate. Compact forms are from exposed east-coast headlands, the others from forests; check nursery labels carefully. Leaves are about 2 cm long. The white or, rarely, pink flowerheads persist for most of the year. With good drainage and near to full sun both forms make excellent rockery plants. Frost hardy. Propagate from cuttings.

Pink Banjine • *Pimelea rosea*   *Zones:* A B C G
This small open, slender bush to 60 cm high by 30 cm across is a useful rockery plant. It has narrow leaves, about 1.5 cm long, and heads of deep pink, occasionally pale, flowers at the ends of branches in spring. Good drainage and full sun or part shade. Frost hardy. Propagate from cuttings.

Saltbushes

Saltbushes occur in arid and semi-arid areas of the world where soils are salty. Some species occur near the sea. Leaves are often grey and succulent with a salty flavour. The flowers of most species are insignificant. Drought- and frost-resistant, they are used to revegetate saline areas.

Old Man Saltbush • *Atriplex nummularia*   *Zones:* H
An erect shrub to 3 m high by 2 m across with roundish grey leaves about 3 cm in diameter. It is often grown as a shelter plant around inland homesteads where it may form a hedge and can be pruned. Prefers well-drained sunny sites. Propagate from cuttings.

• Pink Rice Flower *Pimelea ferruginea*

• Pink Banjine *Pimelea rosea*

• Slender Rice Flower *Pimelea linifolia*

• Old Man Saltbush *Atriplex nummularia*

Spiny Saltbush · *Rhagodia spinescens*   *Zones:* A B c G H

Despite the common name, most forms of this plant available in nurseries do not have spines. This variable shrub may be upright to 1.5 m, or spreading to 1.5 m across and less than 60 cm high. In this form it makes a good hardy ground cover. The silvery grey leaves are diamond-shaped and up to 2 cm long, making a pleasant colour contrast with surrounding greenery. This plant will withstand considerable neglect. Good drainage and full sun are required. Frost hardy. Propagate from cuttings.

Sedges

Australia has many species of sedge, most of which have little horticultural potential. A few are very ornamental, however, and will enhance the surrounds of pools or wet areas where little else will survive.

Leafy Flat Sedge · *Cyperus lucidus*   *Zones:* A B c D G

This robust tufted plant has narrow leaves to 80 cm long and flowering stems to 1 m with umbrella-like heads of green flowers in spring. It is hardy in most soils providing ample water is available. Full sun or part shade are suitable. Frost hardy. Propagate by division.

Feather Rush · *Baloskion tetraphyllum*   *Zones:* A B D G

A tufted plant grown for its handsome, bright green, feathery foliage to 1 m high, the Feather Rush has insignificant small brown flowers near the tips of the leaves. The foliage is sometimes seen in florist shops. It is an excellent plant for the edges of ornamental pools. Hardy in damp situations in full sun or part shade. May be slightly frost tender. Propagation is difficult from seed but may be easier by division.

She-oaks

She-oaks are also commonly known as casuarinas. There are about 90 species in four genera, 66 occurring naturally in Australia. They are easy to recognise, with their foliage consisting of small branchlets ('needles'), their leaves reduced to tiny scales around the stems. Male and female flowers may be on different plants. The female flowers produce the typical 'nuts' or cones.

Forest Oak · *Allocasuarina torulosa*   *Zones:* A B c D E G

This small hardy shelter tree to 15 m high has rough corky bark, barrel-shaped cones about 3 cm long and drooping foliage that reddens in cold climates, providing interesting foliage contrast. Most soils and full sun or part shade. Frost hardy. Propagate from seed.

• Spiny Saltbush *Rhagodia spinescens*

• Leafy Flat Sedge *Cyperus lucidus*

• Feather Rush *Baloskion tetraphyllum*

• Forest Oak *Allocasuarina torulosa*

Horsetail Oak · *Casuarina equisetifolia* ssp. *incana*   *Zones:* B D E F

This is a tree of the seaside where its weeping greyish branchlets make a pleasing sight. It grows to about 9 m with an open habit. The cones are cylindrical and about 2 cm long. It is a excellent plant for sandy soils near the sea. Prefers full sun. Probably frost tender. Propagate from seed.

Swamp Oak · *Casuarina glauca*   *Zones:* A B C D G

A tall tree which may be best used in parks and large properties, the Swamp Oak will reach 20 m in good conditions. The 'needles' are dark green and the branches slightly pendulous. The cones are cylindrical and 1–2 cm long. This tree will grow in most soils and aspects. Frost hardy. Propagate from seed.

Sundews

 Sundews are 'insect-eating' plants. They are covered with small sticky hairs on which insects are trapped and slowly digested by the chemicals exuded by the plant and thus turned into nutrients. These plants are frequently available through the Australian Carnivorous Plant Society, which produces a newsletter with advertisements for plant suppliers. It also has a seed bank for members. Sundews belong to the genus Drosera, which has more than 50 species native to Australia. They grow in damp situations where there is much insect activity. Many are readily cultivated in either a bog garden or in pots.

Forked Sundew · *Drosera binata*   *Zones:* A B C D G

On this plant, long light green leaves to 20 cm arise from a central crown. The ends are divided once or twice into narrow segments. The leaf stalks and the terminal forks are covered with short sticky hairs. White flowers about 2.5 cm in diameter are borne on an erect stem to 50 cm in summer. Grow in a peaty mix that is not allowed to dry out. Pots should be stood in a saucer of water which is emptied from time to time. Moderately high light is best. Sensitive to heavy frosts. Propagate from seed.

Common Sundew · *Drosera spatulata*   *Zones:* A B C D G

Probably Australia's most common sundew, this plant develops a small rosette of leaves that are often reddish. Each leaf is about 2.5 cm long, enlarged towards the tip and covered with sticky hairs. A small flower spike arises from the centre of the rosette in spring with several tiny pink or white flowers. Grow in containers with a peat-based soil mix and keep moist by standing the pot in a saucer of water. Empty the saucer from time to time to remove accumulated salts. Keep the container in good light. Sensitive to heavy frosts. Propagate from seed.

• Horsetail Oak *Casuarina equisetifolia* ssp. *incana*

• Swamp Oak *Casuarina glauca*

• Forked Sundew *Drosera binata*

• Common Sundew *Drosera spatulata*

Tea Trees and Their Relatives

The term 'tea tree' applies to a large collection of plants that mostly occur naturally only in Australia, and from which the early settlers made a drink resembling tea by soaking the leaves in hot water. They are shrubs or small trees with five-petalled flowers varying in colour from white through pinks to rarely red. Some have highly aromatic foliage, others have attractive bark. In the garden they are hardy in an open sunny position and tolerant of most soils, except the very wet, although one or two will grow in running water. Regular light pruning after flowering will improve their general shape. Webbing caterpillars, which build a web-like mass amongst the foliage, may trouble several species. These are best controlled by physically removing the web mass and squashing it. The true tea trees belong to the genus Leptospermum but a number of their relatives are look-alikes and are included here because of the superficial similarity of their flowers and the fact that their culture is also similar.

Midgen · *Austromyrtus dulcis*   Zones: A B C D G

Often used as a ground cover, this shrub will reach 50 cm high by 1 m across. The dark green leaves are lance-shaped and about 3 cm long, with the new growth being red. White flowers are produced in summer. The small greyish fruits are edible and sweet. It grows well in most soils but appreciates ample water. Frost hardy. Propagate from cuttings.

Howie's Feathertips or Miniature Baeckea ·
Babingtonia 'Howie's Feathertips'   Zones: B C D G

This is such a wonderful foliage plant that it makes one want to pat it. It forms a smooth rounded shrub about 1 m by 1 m, dotted with small white flowers in summer. No pruning is necessary to maintain its tight shape. It will grow in most soils in a sunny situation. Frost hardy. Propagate from cuttings.

Short-leaved Broombush · *Babingtonia behrii*   Zones: C H

Native to semi-arid areas, Short-leaved Broombush is an ideal choice for a dry spot. It is an upright shrub to 2 m high by 1 m across with fine leaves and small white flowers in spring and summer. It is used as a filler flower for floral arrangements. It will grow in most soils in a sunny situation. Frost hardy. Propagate from cuttings.

Walpole Wax · *Chamelaucium floriferum*   Zones: A G

This plant develops a bushy habit and reaches 2 m high by 1.5 m across. The flowers are white, about 1.2 cm in diameter, and borne profusely in spring. It is used as a cut flower. Requires excellent drainage and full sun. May be sensitive to heavy frosts. Propagate from cuttings.

• Midgen *Austromyrtus dulcis*

• **Howie's Feathertips or Miniature Baeckea**
Babingtonia 'Howie's Feathertips'

• **Short-leaved Broombush** *Babingtonia behrii*

• **Walpole Wax** *Chamelaucium floriferum*

Geraldton Wax · *Chamelaucium uncinatum*   *Zones:* A C G H

Well known in cultivation and used extensively as a commercial cut flower, this species is best grown in areas with low summer humidity. It will grow to 3 m high by 2 m across. Regular pruning will keep it compact. The colour of the spring flowers varies from white through pinks to purple. The cultivar 'Purple Pride' is very dark. Excellent drainage and a sunny site are recommended. Slightly frost tender. Propagate from cuttings.

TEA TREES

Coastal Tea Tree · *Leptospermum laevigatum*   *Zones:* A B

The great value of this species is its resistance to salt spray. It can be used in coastal gardens as a barrier to protect sensitive plants from damaging salt-laden winds. Unfortunately, it has been used in great numbers outside its natural areas of occurrence to stabilise dunes that have been mined or otherwise made bare. In these cases it has become a weed and is preventing natural revegetation taking place. This large shrub will reach 5 m high by 4 m across. The flowers are white and are borne in spring and early summer. Frost hardy. Propagate from seed or cuttings.

Hillside Wild May · *Leptospermum luehmannii*   *Zones:* B D

An upright shrub, Hillside Wild May usually develops several trunks covered with smooth light brown bark peeling annually in long ribbons. Its white flowers appear in summer. Ensure that its colourful trunks are exposed to view as they make an attractive landscape feature. Good drainage and a sunny site are recommended. Sensitive to heavy frosts. Propagate from seed or cuttings.

Weeping Tea Tree ·
Leptospermum madidum ssp. *sativum*   *Zones:* D E F

This tropical species has graceful pendulous branches and resembles a small weeping willow. It reaches 3 m high by 3 m across and has tiny white flowers. Use it as a feature plant for its superb form. Will not withstand frosts. Propagate from seed or cuttings.

Lemon-scented Tea Tree · *Leptospermum petersonii*   *Zones:* B D G

The fresh lemon scent from the foliage of this plant has been used commercially as a flavouring agent; in the garden it provides a pleasant surprise when one brushes past the branches. It will reach up to 4 m high by 3 m across, with small white flowers appearing in summer. Hardy in most soils and situations. Will not tolerate heavy frosts. Propagate from seed or cuttings.

Pink Cascade · *Leptospermum* 'Pink Cascade'   *Zones:* A B C D G

Producing masses of pink flowers from spring to early summer, this attractive cultivar rarely exceeds 1 m high by 1.5 m across. Its flowers are about 1 cm in diameter. Hardy in most soils in full sun or part shade. Frost hardy. Propagate from cuttings.

• Geraldton Wax *Chamelaucium uncinatum*

• Coastal Tea Tree *Leptospermum laevigatum*

• Hillside Wild May *Leptospermum luehmannii*

• Weeping Tea Tree *Leptospermum madidum*
ssp. *sativum*

• Lemon-scented Tea Tree *Leptospermum petersonii*

• Pink Cascade *Leptospermum* 'Pink Cascade'

Pacific Beauty · *Leptospermum* 'Pacific Beauty'   *Zones:* A B C D G

This cultivar with weeping branches may spread to 2 m with a height of 1.5 m. Producing masses of white flowers 1.5 cm in diameter, it will begin to flower in early spring in northern areas but several weeks later in areas where frosts are more common. Hardy in most soils in full sun or part shade. Frost hardy. Propagate from cuttings.

Round-leaf Tea Tree · *Leptospermum rotundifolium*   *Zones:* A B C G

This species forms a bushy shrub to 2 m by 2 m with attractive shiny green, round leaves and pink flowers, about 2.5 cm in diameter, starting in late spring. It is a very reliable, hardy plant for temperate zones but does not flower well in the subtropics or tropics. Hardy in most soils in full sun or part shade. Frost hardy. Propagate from seed or cuttings.

Julie Ann · *Leptospermum* 'Julie Ann'   *Zones:* A B C G

This is a semi-prostrate form of the Round-leaf Tea Tree which may reach 30 cm in height by 70 cm across, displaying showy pink flowers in late spring. Hardy in most soils in full sun or part shade. Frost hardy. Propagate from cuttings.

Creeping Tea Tree · *Leptospermum rupestre*   *Zones:* A C

This plant is completely prostrate, clinging to rocks in its natural Tasmanian habitat. Its flowers are white and appear mainly in summer. It makes an excellent rockery plant for areas that experience hard frosts. Hardy in most soils in full sun or part shade. Propagate from seed or cuttings.

Trigger Plants

 Trigger plants belong to the genus Stylidium, *which has more than 100 species, all endemic to Australia. Few are available commercially so only one is included here. Probably the best known, it is widespread in eastern and southern Australia. The common name is derived from the pollination method. The anthers and the stigma are combined in an irritable organ called the column. When an insect alights on the base of this column, it reacts like a trigger and hits the insect on the back, depositing a quantity of pollen. The insect then carries the pollen to the next flower. The triggers are only reactive on warm sunny days.*

Grass-leaved Trigger Plant · *Stylidium graminifolium*   *Zones:* A B C D G

This tufted plant varies greatly in leaf and flower size and colour. The grass-like leaves may be 5–25 cm long, and the pale pink to deep magenta flowers are borne on an erect stem 20–40 cm tall in spring. A well-drained sunny position is recommended. It makes an ideal rockery plant. Frost hardy. Propagate from seed.

• Pacific Beauty *Leptospermum* 'Pacific Beauty'

• Round-leaf Tea Tree *Leptospermum rotundifolium*

• Creeping Tea Tree *Leptospermum rupestre*

• Julie Ann *Leptospermum* 'Julie Ann'

• Grass-leaved Trigger Plant *Stylidium graminifolium*

Veronicas

 The three frost-hardy perennials listed here all have flowers in varying shades of blue. They all require cutting back after flowering to allow the new growth room to shoot.

Derwent Speedwell · *Derwentia derwentiana*   *Zones:* A B C

This plant is a tall perennial with a number of 1 m stems rising from the permanent root-stock each growing season. The toothed leaves vary from 5 to 20 cm long. White or pale blue flowers are borne at the end of the stems in summer. Cut back the old season growths in late winter. Most soils and aspects are suitable. Frost hardy. Propagate from cuttings or by division.

Digger's Speedwell · *Derwentia perfoliata*   *Zones:* A B C

This perennial grows to 60 cm high and spreads to 1 m with arching stems and broad grey-green leaves that clasp the stems. Nodding sprays of bright blue flowers are borne at the stem ends in summer. Cut back the old stems when flowering is complete. Prefers a well-drained site in half shade. Frost hardy. Propagate from cuttings or by division.

Tasmanian Veronica · *Veronica formosa*   *Zones:* A B C

With a similar habit to the two speedwells, this plant has small dark green leaves and stems to about 60 cm high. Light blue flowers are borne in spring and summer. Cut back stems when flowers are finished. Most soils and aspects are suitable. Frost hardy. Propagate from cuttings or by division.

• Derwent Speedwell *Derwentia derwentiana*   • Digger's Speedwell *Derwentia perfoliata*

• Tasmanian Veronica *Veronica formosa*

Waratahs

 The well-known Sydney Waratah is the floral emblem of New South Wales. In recent years considerable attention has been paid to its development as a commercial cut flower and it is now an important export. Plant breeders have made selections of clones with different characteristics and as a result various cultivars are now available. Some have smaller flowers, some have white tips to the stigmas, some have green bracts and some have a later flowering time. Although waratahs have a reputation for being difficult to grow, if you follow the directions given below for the Sydney Waratah you should have success with the cultivars mentioned.

Sydney Waratah · *Telopea speciosissima*   *Zones:* A B C

Occurring on the Hawkesbury sandstone country around Sydney and the Blue Mountains, this species forms a multi-trunked shrub to 3 m in height. The leaves are toothed and about 18 cm long and the large red flowers are borne at the ends of stems in spring. The flowerhead is surrounded by petal-like bracts that vary in size and are usually red. This desirable species requires excellent drainage and a light soil supplied with a good mulch of compost or leaf litter. Accepts both full sun or a little shade. Regular cutting of the flowers encourages branching and serves as a form of pruning to produce more flowers the following season. Fertilise with a low phosphorus fertiliser. Frost hardy. Propagate from seed or cuttings.

Corroboree · *Telopea* 'Corroboree'   *Zones:* A B C

This cultivar, reaching about 3 m high, is a hybrid between the Sydney Waratah and the Monga Waratah, *Telopea mongaensis*, from the southern highlands of New South Wales. It was bred to produce a smaller flower with few bracts. Growing conditions are the same as for the Sydney Waratah. Frost hardy. Propagate from cuttings.

Wirrimbirra White · *Telopea* 'Wirrimbirra White'   *Zones:* A B C

This naturally occurring white-flowered variety of the Sydney Waratah was discovered some years ago south of Sydney and is now available in nurseries. It makes a lovely contrast when grown close to the red variety. It is generally smaller than the others mentioned, rarely exceeding 2 m high. Growing conditions are the same. Frost hardy. Propagate from cuttings.

• Sydney Waratah *Telopea speciosissima*   • Corroboree *Telopea* 'Corroboree'

• Wirrimbirra White *Telopea* 'Wirrimbirra White'

Water Plants

 A water feature is always a lovely addition to the garden. The tinkling sound of a small fountain or a waterfall improves it still further, adding to the peace and serenity of a garden. Many of the plants mentioned in this book may be used for the pool surrounds, but those in this section are for use in the pool itself. They are truly aquatic. Their cultivation depends a little on the pool construction but generally, if the pool is lined or constructed in concrete, they may be grown in containers and sunk carefully into the water. Use a heavy soil mix with a little animal manure added to it and cover the surface with a layer of coarse sand to prevent the soil mix from clouding the water. Once the plant is positioned in the container, lower it very carefully into the water, allowing the air bubbles to escape gradually from the soil. Repot each year or two.

Foxtail · *Ceratophyllum demersum*   Zones: **A B** D **E F** G

This little plant does not produce roots but floats completely submerged in the water. It has dainty foliage with whorled divided leaves and insignificant flowers. It will not stand really cold water. Plants may be anchored in the pool with rocks. Goldfish may eat the leaves but it grows quickly. This plant is usually available from aquarium shops. Propagate by division.

Water Fern · *Ceratopteris thalictroides*   Zones: **D E F**

This handsome fern will root in the mud at the bottom of the pool or float on the surface with its fronds exposed. The fronds are a soft green and divided several times. Plantlets are produced on the fronds and are the best method of propagation. Often available from aquarium shops, this plant is only suitable for use in the subtropics or tropics, or a heated aquarium elsewhere.

Water Isotome · *Isotoma fluviatilis*   Zones: **A** B C D **G**

This prostrate plant will grow in water or at the water's edge with its creeping stems reaching the water. The tiny leaves are only about 1 cm long and the blue star-shaped spring flowers are about the same size. It is probably best to plant it at the pool edge and let it spread into the water. Frost hardy. Propagate by division, as it roots at the nodes.

Nardoo · *Marsilea drummondii*   *All Zones*

Related to ferns, this species will grow at the pool edge or in the water as a floating plant where it looks its best. Its leaves are reminiscent of a four-leaved clover, and tend to be a reddish colour in full sunlight. It produces its fruiting bodies only when it is on dry land. Aborigines collected these spore bodies and crushed them to produce a flour rich in carbohydrates. Frost hardy. Propagate by division of the aquatic stems.

• Foxtail *Ceratophyllum demersum*

• Water Fern *Ceratopteris thalictroides*

• Water Isotome *Isotoma fluviatilis*

• Nardoo *Marsilea drummondii*

Sacred Lotus • *Nelumbo nucifera*   *Zones:* D E F

This beautiful plant needs water to about 1 m deep. Its large circular leaves, about 30–80 cm in diameter, are held 20–30 cm above the water surface. The huge pink or white flowers, 20 cm in diameter, are produced from late winter to summer. They are followed by brown cup-shaped fruits with holes in the top holding the seeds. Unfortunately this plant must have warm water conditions and full sun to survive, limiting its range. It is available from water-plant nurseries. Pot in a large container using a rich mixture. Very frost tender. Propagate from division of rootstock before new growth begins.

Giant Water Lily • *Nymphaea gigantea*   *Zones:* B D E F G

Australia has several species of native water lily. This one has large circular floating leaves edged with small teeth. The flowers, 25 cm in diameter, are held above the water surface in summer and may be white, blue or pink. Although frost tender, this species will grow well in the subtropics. Full sun is best. Pot in a rich mixture. Propagate by division of the rhizome.

Wavy Marshwort • *Nymphoides crenata*   *Zones:* A B D G

The small floating leaves of this species are about 10 cm in diameter with scalloped margins. Roots develop just under the leaves at a stem joint. The fringed flowers are yellow and about 3.5 cm in diameter, appearing in spring and summer. While it prefers warm conditions, plants occur in the wild as far south as Victoria. Plant in containers or let the plant root in the mud at the bottom of the pond. Frost tender. Propagate by division.

Water Snowflake • *Nymphoides indica*   *Zones:* D E F

This species has much larger floating leaves than the Wavy Marshwort. They are circular and up to 30 cm in diameter. The fringed flowers are white. It will survive in water up to 2 m deep and needs full sun to flower well from early summer to autumn. It is essentially a plant for the tropics or subtropics as frost will kill it. Propagate by division.

Swamp Lily • *Otellia ovalifolia*   *Zones:* A B D E G H

Growing in water to 30 cm deep, this species has oval floating leaves and narrower strap-like submerged leaves. The three-petalled white flowers float on the surface. They are about 5 cm in diameter and produced in summer and autumn. Plant in a container in a well-fertilised mixture. Frost hardy. Propagate from seed.

Ribbonweed • *Vallisneria nana*   *Zones:* A B D E F G H

With its long strands of ribbon-like leaves sometimes reaching 1 m, this plant is an excellent oxygenator for a pool. In moving water it tends to go with the flow and when the water is clear has a pleasing appearance. The flowers are insignificant. Plant in a container in a well-fertilised mixture. It is also a useful aquarium plant. Frost hardy. Propagate by division.

• **Sacred Lotus** *Nelumbo nucifera*

• **Giant Water Lily** *Nymphaea gigantea*

• **Wavy Marshwort** *Nymphoides crenata*

• **Water Snowflake** *Nymphoides indica*

• **Swamp Lily** *Otellia ovalifolia*

• **Ribbonweed** *Vallisneria nana*

Wattles

Wattle is the common name of members of the genus Acacia. *With almost 1000 species native to Australia, it is the largest genus of our flora. There are few environments where a wattle does not occur. They are found in the arid interior, the high mountains, on the coast and even in rainforest. They may be shrubs or trees and generally adapt well to cultivation providing the proper selection of species is made for a particular area. Most have yellow or cream flowers, which may appear as round balls or elongated rod-like spikes. After flowering, the seeds develop in a pod, the shape varying considerably with the species. The seeds have a very tough coat and germination will only occur once this coat is cracked to allow water to enter. The easiest way to do this is to pour boiling water over the seed and allow it to stand overnight before sowing. Most wattles prefer a sunny position in reasonably well-drained soil. Although many are very quick growing, their useful life span is often only about 8–10 years.*

Coastal Myall • *Acacia binervia*   *Zones:* B D
A small to medium-sized tree, reaching 15 m high, this species is fast growing in a frost-free area. It is very bushy and with its silvery grey foliage makes an excellent screen plant. The golden flowers are borne in rods about 5 cm long in spring. It will accept some shade but prefers full sun. Most soils are suitable.

Cootamundra Wattle • *Acacia baileyana*   *Zones:* A B C
This large bushy shrub may reach 8 m high by 8 m across and is very well known for its brilliant display of golden flowers in late winter in temperate areas. It will grow in warmer climates but will not flower well. The feathery blue-grey leaves are attractive and the sprays of small ball-shaped flowers are prolific. Full sun and most soils are suitable. Frost hardy. Take care that the plant does not escape and become a weed, as it has this potential.

Barrier Range Wattle • *Acacia beckleri*   *Zones:* A B C H
A small to medium-sized shrub 2–3 m high, this wattle has thick leaves to 15 cm long and particularly large, golden yellow ball-shaped flowers in late winter and early spring. It is drought-resistant and requires a well-drained soil. Frost hardy.

Snowy River Wattle • *Acacia boormanii*   *Zones:* A B C
A rounded shrub to 2–3 m in height, with grey-green leaves to 7 cm long, this fine species makes a wonderful spring display with its golden ball flowers. It is best suited to temperate areas and requires a reasonably well-drained soil in full sun. Frost hardy.

• Coastal Myall *Acacia binervia*

• Barrier Range Wattle *Acacia beckleri*

• Cootamundra Wattle *Acacia baileyana*

• Snowy River Wattle *Acacia boormanii*

West Wyalong Wattle • *Acacia cardiophylla* *Zones:* A B C H

A spreading medium-sized shrub to 2 m high by 3 m across, this species has light green feathery leaves and sprays of bright yellow ball flowers in spring. Good drainage is essential as leaf drop may occur on poorly drained soils. Grow in full sun. Frost hardy.

Flat-stem Wattle • *Acacia complanata* *Zones:* B D E

This medium-sized spreading shrub to 3 m in height has flattened stems and slightly reddish bark, with light green leaves about 10 cm long. The yellow ball-shaped flowers appear in spring and often also after rain. This wattle, hardy in most soils, is an asset in subtropical and tropical gardens as flowers frequently appear in the rainy season. Probably frost tender.

Broad-leaf Mulga • *Acacia craspedocarpa* *Zones:* B D G H

Although this erect shrub comes from Western Australia, it seems to thrive in the subtropics of the east coast provided it has good drainage. It grows to 2.5 m high by 1.5 m across with broad grey-green leaves to 2 cm long. Small, bright yellow rod-shaped flowers about 1.5 cm long appear throughout the year. It has flattened grey pods. Frost hardy.

Knife-leaf Wattle • *Acacia cultriformis* *Zones:* A B C G H

This erect shrub will reach 2.5 m high by 2 m across. It has grey triangular leaves about 2 cm long and produces masses of bright yellow ball flowers in spring. This popular wattle will accept very dry conditions. Most soils are suitable and full sun is recommended. Frost hardy.

Drummond's Wattle • *Acacia drummondii* *Zones:* A C G

Although variable in size, the typical form of this species is a small shrub usually less than 1 m high by 1.5 m across. It has neat compound leaves and golden rod-shaped flowers in spring. It must have good drainage but will accept some shade or full sun. This is one wattle that can be propagated from cuttings. Frost tender.

Elephant Ear Wattle • *Acacia dunnii* *Zones:* F H

This large open shrub grows to 4 m high by 2 m across and has the largest leaves of any wattle. They are grey, broad and up to 45 cm long. It has white stems. The golden ball flowers are also large, about 2 cm in diameter, and borne in conspicuous sprays for much of the year. It will accept very dry conditions and is frost tender. Full sun and good drainage are important.

Fringed Wattle • *Acacia fimbriata* *Zones:* A B C D

This wattle is a large bushy tree that has been much used to vegetate road verges on the east coast. It will reach 7 m high by 6 m across, with narrow lance-shaped leaves with tiny hairs fringing the margins. The fragrant yellow ball flowers are borne prolifically in spring. Hardy in most soils and aspects. Frost hardy.

• West Wyalong Wattle *Acacia cardiophylla*

• Flat-stem Wattle *Acacia complanata*

• Broad-leaf Mulga *Acacia craspedocarpa*

• Knife-leaf Wattle *Acacia cultriformis*

• Drummond's Wattle *Acacia drummondii*

• Elephant Ear Wattle *Acacia dunnii*

• Fringed Wattle *Acacia fimbriata*

Soap • *Acacia holosericea* Zones: D E F H

This large open shrub to 3 m high by 3 m across has stiff, erect, grey leaves to 20 cm long. The golden yellow spring flowers are rod-shaped and about 5–6 cm long. On maturity the twisted seed pods are retained on the shrub in clusters. They are sticky and when rubbed on the hands tend to remove dirt, hence the common name. Regular pruning after flowering improves the shape. The plant is hardy in most soils and full sun. Frost tender.

Zig-zag Wattle • *Acacia macradenia* Zones: D E F H

This open, slightly pendulous shrub will reach 6 m in height and has unusual zig-zag branches that change direction between leaf nodes. The leaves are lance-shaped and about 10 cm long. Bright yellow ball flowers are produced in sprays in early spring. This is a good plant for warm dry situations. Frost tender.

Blackwood • *Acacia melanoxylon* Zones: A B C D

A fast-growing tall tree, Blackwood is useful for a quick shelter-belt planting on rural properties. The leaves are lance-shaped and about 14 cm long and the ball-shaped flowers are cream and may appear several times each year. Most soils and aspects are suitable. In warmer climates, plants are prone to borer attack. Frost hardy.

Mountford's Wattle • *Acacia mountfordiae* Zones: D F H

This spreading shrub is best suited to tropical gardens. It will grow to 2 m high by 3 m across. It has blue-green, almost round leaves about 3 cm across and rod-shaped golden spring flowers to 3 cm long. It requires very good drainage and full sun. Frost tender.

Golden Wreath Wattle • *Acacia saligna* Zones: A C G

A small tree or large shrub from Western Australia, this wattle quickly reaches 8–10 m in height with a spreading crown. The long leaves are up to 20 cm long and 5–20 mm wide, and the golden ball flowers, about 1 cm in diameter, are borne prolifically in sprays in spring. Hardy in most soils and aspects. Frost hardy. Care should be taken that this species does not escape from cultivation when grown on the east coast, as it has weed potential.

Coastal Wattle • *Acacia longifolia* ssp. *sophorae* Zones: A B C D

This excellent coastal wattle has been used for stabilising sand dunes on the east coast in areas disturbed by mining. It forms a spreading shrub to 2–3 m high by 4 m across and is very resistant to salt spray. Yellow rod-shaped flowers 2–3 cm long in spring. Frost hardy.

Mudgee Wattle • *Acacia spectabilis* Zones: A B C

A large shrub to 6 m in height, with lacy blue-green compound leaves and greyish stems, this wattle carries masses of golden ball flowers in spring. The flattened pods are purplish. It is well worth growing in temperate areas. Most soils and a sunny site. Frost hardy.

• Soap *Acacia holosericea*

• **Zig-zag Wattle** *Acacia macradenia*

• Blackwood *Acacia melanoxylon*

• Mountford's Wattle *Acacia mountfordiae*

• **Golden Wreath Wattle** *Acacia saligna*

• **Coastal Wattle** *Acacia longifolia* ssp. *sophorae*

• **Mudgee Wattle** *Acacia spectabilis*

Weeping Boree · *Acacia vestita*
Zones: A B c H

This beautiful shrub will reach about 3 m high by 5 m across with pendulous branches and grey-green, hairy, oval leaves to 2 cm long. The golden ball flowers are borne in spring. This is an outstanding shrub for temperate areas but usually does not flower well in subtropical coastal climates. Most soils and aspects are suitable. Frost hardy.

Wax Flowers and Their Relatives

'Wax flower' is perhaps a confusing common name for this group of plants as the name also applies to the Geraldton Wax, which is quite unrelated. They might be better known as 'eriostemons'—but further confusion lies here as the botanical name Eriostemon *is now restricted to just two species, neither of which is covered in this book. So we have stayed with wax flower.*

Small Crowea · *Crowea exalata*
Zones: A B c G

This small shrub reaches 70 cm high by 50 cm wide with narrow leaves to 4 cm. Star-shaped flowers, 2 cm in diameter, vary in colour from white to deep pink and are borne from summer to autumn. This very decorative plant requires a reasonably well-drained soil, good mulch and full sun or part shade. Flowers when other blooms are scarce, and the blooms are good for cutting. Frost hardy. Propagate from cuttings.

Crowea · *Crowea saligna*
Zones: A B c G

A little larger than the Small Crowea, this plant will reach 1 m high with longer elliptical leaves to 5 cm. The star-shaped flowers are also larger, 3.5 cm across, and borne in autumn and winter. Cultivation requirements are similar. It is also used as a cut flower. Frost hardy. Propagate from cuttings. A hybrid, *Crowea* 'Festival', is also available.

Forest Phebalium · *Phebalium squamulosum*
Zones: A B c

This is a very variable species with several forms available. Most often it is a medium-sized shrub, 2–3 m in height, with narrow or elliptical leaves of varying length. The yellow or cream flowers are well displayed, borne in clusters at the ends of branches in spring. Good drainage is important and plants benefit from a good mulch of leaf litter. Accepts some shade but prefers full sun. Frost hardy. Propagate from cuttings.

Long-leaf Wax Flower · *Philotheca myoporoides*
(formerly *Eriostemon myoporoides*)
Zones: A B c D G

Very well known in cultivation, this beautiful shrub is hardy in most soils and aspects. It is variable in height but generally reaches about 1.5 m high by 1 m across. The star-shaped flowers are pink in bud and open white. They are about 1.5 cm in diameter and appear from late winter to spring. Frost hardy. Propagate from cuttings.

• **Weeping Boree** *Acacia vestita*

• **Small Crowea** *Crowea exalata*

• **Crowea** *Crowea saligna*

• **Forest Phebalium** *Phebalium squamulosum*

• **Long-leaf Wax Flower** *Philotheca myoporoides*

Willow Myrtles

The common name 'willow myrtle' or 'myrtle' applies to several Western Australian plants in the genus Agonis. *They are hardy trees and shrubs that do well in temperate areas on both sides of the country.*

Willow Myrtle or Willow Peppermint • *Agonis flexuosa*   Zones: A C G

A handsome weeping tree to 14 m in height, this plant is resistant to salt spray and grows best in sandy soils. It is not unlike the Weeping Willow, *Salix babylonica*, in character, but does not share the invasive root system of that species. The white flowers are borne in clusters in late spring and summer. Slightly frost tender. Propagate from seed.

Native Cedar or Juniper Myrtle • *Agonis juniperina*   Zones: A B C G

An erect shrub to 5 m high by 2 m across, with a columnar habit, at least when young. The dark green leaves are about 1 cm long. White flowers are borne in globular heads at the ends of short branchlets. It flowers mainly in autumn, but also at other times. Flowering branches are often picked and dried for indoor decoration. Hardy in most soils and aspects. Resistant to both frost and salt spray. Propagate from seed or cuttings.

Woody Pears

These belong to the protea family, which is spread across the Southern Hemisphere. There are six species, all Australian, with two in the south-west and the others on the east coast. They require excellent drainage.

Woody Pear • *Xylomelum pyriforme*   Zones: A B

This unusual plant forms a large shrub to 4 m high by 2–3 m across, with narrow elliptical leaves to 20 cm. The young growth is red. The creamy white flowers are borne in short spikes in spring and followed by large pear-like woody fruits covered with a grey felty coating. They are about 10 cm long and popular in floral decorations. Requires excellent drainage and part shade. Slightly frost tender. Propagate from seed.

Western Woody Pear • *Xylomelum angustifolium*   Zones: A G

An open shrub to 3 m in height with narrow pointed leaves to 15 cm, this plant has creamy white flowers in spikes to 10 cm long in summer. The fruits are narrower than those of the previous species but borne more prolifically, and are exported in considerable quantity for the cut flower market. Very good drainage in sandy soils is required. May be sensitive to heavy frosts. Propagate from seed.

• Willow Myrtle or Willow Peppermint
Agonis flexuosa

• Native Cedar *Agonis juniperina*

• Woody Pear *Xylomelum pyriforme*

• Western Woody Pear *Xylomelum angustifolium*